Still Catholic

After All These *FEARS*

ALSO BY ED STIVENDER

Book

Raised Catholic (Can You Tell?)

Videotapes

The Kingdom of Heaven Is Like a Party
Raised Catholic (Can You Tell?)

Audiotapes

Once ...
Some of My Best Friends Are Kids
Raised Catholic (Can You Tell?)
Yankee Come Home

Fr Jean –
Still Catholic, are you?
I could tell!

Still Catholic

After All These FEARS

Nolite Timere !

Ed Stivender

ED STIVENDER

August House Publishers, Inc.
LITTLE ROCK

Printed in the United States of America

10 9 8 7 6 5 4 3 2 1 HC
10 9 8 7 6 5 4 3 2 1 PB

LIBRARY OF CONGRESS CATALOGING-IN-PUBLICATION DATA

Stivender, Ed, 1946–
Still Catholic after all these fears / Ed Stivender.
p.   cm.
ISBN 0-87483-403-1 (alk. paper : hb)
ISBN 0-87483-483-X (alk. paper : pbk)
1. Stivender, Ed, 1946– . 2. Catholic—United States—Biography. I. Title.
BX4705.S8264A3   1995
282'.092—dc20   94-49236

First Edition, 1995
First Paperback Edition, 1996

Executive editor: Liz Parkhurst
Editorial assistants: Debbie Tarvin, Nancy King
Best boy: Ed Stivender
Cover design: Harvill Ross Studios Ltd.
Cover photograph: Seymour Mednick

The paper used in this publication meets the minimum requirements
of the American National Standards for Information Sciences—
permanence of Paper for Printed Library Materials, ANSI.48-1984

AUGUST HOUSE, INC.   PUBLISHERS   LITTLE ROCK

To my father, Alvey Vernon Stivender, USN—
a view from the parish side.

Teach us to care and not to care,
teach us to sit still.

T.S. Eliot, "Ash Wednesday"

Acknowledgments

I'd like to thank all my old classmates who surfaced since the publication of my first book, *Raised Catholic (Can You Tell?)*. Their comments and corrections of my memory have been very helpful in developing this second batch of stories. These include Diane Tasca, Kathy Hughes, Jackie Woulfe, Joe Wusinich, Joe Lang, John Volk, Carolyn Reese, Jeanette Leonetti, Kathy Consalvi, Mary Spellman, Julie Vellutello Keyser, and Terry Hartnett Fuhs, to name a few.

I'd also like to thank Sister Patrick Mary for letting me take her (old) name in vain (again). The temper of the character portrayed in the first story here is much shorter than that of the real person, as her friends and sisters know.

I had hoped that the first book would offend no one mentioned by name, and I apologize to M.C. and her family for my insensitivity. In this volume, I am a little wary of using real names, especially when there is an issue of conflict, or where the Narrative Imperative yields improbable developments. To quote Quince in *A Midsummer Night's Dream*, "If we offend ... it is with our good will."

I'd like to thank the inventor of WordPerfect for making this work easier than the last, and my scriveners, The Write Type of Germantown, for printing the working manuscripts.

Thanks to my college chums Ed Deegan, Lynn Biddle, and Karen Hurley, for their help with the final draft; to Pat Montley, for listening; and to Jan Smith, for her shortbread wisdom.

For Heather Forest's fine ear and George Blood's well-tuned eye, thanks.

Without the organizational skills and kindness of my sister and manager, Nancy Clancy, I wouldn't be able to tie my own virtual shoes, let alone schedule the time to write these stories.

Thanks to Liz Parkhurst for her patience and discernment as I tried to distract her with a liturgical thriller based on my conflict with the liberal parish that royalties enabled me to flee, and her insistence that there was more to my story than one volume.

Thanks to the communities of Germantown Meeting and St. Bridget's Parish, and the Wernersville Jesuit Retreat Center, for space and time for work and worship.

And finally, dear reader, thank you for your attention. Please keep me in your prayers. ❧

Contents

Introduction

*I*f you are raised Catholic, one thing you learn how to do is wrestle. You learn to wrestle with your desires, to wrestle with rules that sometimes seem senseless, to wrestle with doctrines and philosophical concepts that you don't fully understand.

I am glad for the training I received, for this project of writing has been a kind of wrestling match.

I have wrestled with my editor over what to leave in and what to cut out.

I have wrestled with the English language and the attendant demons of gender denotation and connotation.

I have wrestled with the demons that beset any author—writer's block, deadline avoidance, fear of success—but my most interesting bout has been with the Irish Catholic demons of humility and reticence.

You see, we don't talk about ourselves. At least we aren't supposed to, except in the strict confines of the confessional, after which the story is never repeated by the designated listener. But here are twelve stories in which I do talk about myself, and others close to me. These stories are the products of wrestling with my demons—and my angels.

Hopefully I'm working in a fine tradition. Jacob wrestled with an angel and was changed forever; Wicked John, in American folklore, wrestled with the devil and beat him with the help of St. Peter. I have wrestled with an angel, good or bad, and the result is this book.

Now it is your turn. I challenge you to a tag-team match—you and your demons against me and mine. This will be interesting, for as you'll find out in the first story, I have been enlisted in the Church Militant as a Soldier of Christ.

Confirmation: Soldier of Christ

*I*n the early days of the Catholic church, Baptism and Confirmation were received as one sacrament. All Christians at that time were adult converts from either a pagan cult or Judaism, and the water rite of Baptism and the chrisming of Confirmation both happened as part of the Easter Vigil service. When the practice of infant christening gained popularity in the Middle Ages, the sealing with the oil of chrism was delayed until the child was old enough to "confirm" his commitment to the Catholic Faith. In the Archdiocese of Philadelphia in the 1950s it was felt that for the number of years needed to be confirmed, eight was enough. So we began our training for the sacrament in the third grade.

The year before, having reached the "Age of Reason" at age seven, we had received our First Confession and First Holy Communion. We had been attending Sunday, and some of us daily, Mass since then. Most of us also lined up for Confession once a week on Saturday afternoons at 3:30 (perfect timing to squelch any plans for long hikes or extended baseball games).

The theology of Confirmation was a little more complex than that of the other two sacraments—that portion of the catechism posed a greater number of questions as we began our preparation to become "Soldiers of Christ."

American Catholicism, especially the Irish variety that was practiced in the Northeastern dioceses of the United States, had taken on a pugilistic tone from the beginning. Since the Irish were relative latecomers to the States in terms of the overall European immigration, the process of Irish-American acculturation had violent overtones. The Anti-Catholic hostility manifested in the "Know-Nothing" Party riots in the 1840s was on the minds of the bishops who developed the Baltimore Catechism four decades later as a forensic tool for Catholics against their Protestant neighbors.

The Great War in Europe gave the Catholic immigrant a chance to prove his fealty to the flag. The "Fighting 69th" regiment from New York—chaplained by "Fighting Father Duffy," whose statue still graces Times Square—was noted for its bravery on the battlefield. Later, on the football field, the Fighting Irish of Notre Dame would make—and continue to make—their mark.

Add to this the fact that the Cold War pitted the Russians and their atheistic communism against our own Christian country, and it is easy to see the rationale for the moniker of the confirmands as "Soldiers of Christ." Part of the rite of Confirmation was an actual blow on the cheek, ostensibly to test if we were tough enough to be Catholic.

As I approached the sacrament of Confirmation, a real war was being waged in Korea, and horror stories about the torture of Catholic missionaries abounded. With bomb shelters in our neighbors' back yards, televised hearings of the McCarthy investigations, and frequent air raid drills, the world was a very scary place, and we believed we might indeed be called on to defend our faith against a foe far more formidable than any nineteenth-century Know-Nothing.

The games that we played after school and on weekends also reflected the military tenor of the times. In addition to the routine versions of Army played with makeshift stick guns, we also had a favorite we called SAC—Strategic Air Command. This game would start out with a few of us guys relaxing in the swing room, actually the Halls' patio, pretending to drink coffee on an air force base—we were SAC pilots waiting for the signal to prepare for takeoff. The designated flight controller would give the signal—*"beep, beep, beep"*—and we'd all pantomime putting on flight gear and helmets, then become the planes themselves, running across several row house lawns until we got to the small grass hill at the end of the Masons' property, where we launched ourselves into space, rat-a-tat-tat-ing our machine guns as we took off. The hill was just big enough to give us the smallest sense of flying, whereby we would prove ourselves a brave lot and worthy of our Catholic education.

One day Sister Patrick Mary, our third-grade teacher, started Religion class with a question. "Who can tell me the three parts of the Church?"

We had not yet had the question as part of our catechism homework, and my mind was racing to find out a logical answer—"The inside, the outside, and the ...?" But that was only two. One of my classmates, also on the same train of thought, had his hand up.

"Yes, Gerald?" Gerald Mallory had a great imagination. I always enjoyed his attempts; even if they were vain, they were imaginative.

"The inside, the outside, and the basement?" This answer was pretty creative, since our actual church did not have a basement.

"Well, yes, you could say that about a church building, Gerald, but what I mean when I say Church, is the whole people of God, living and dead," said Sister.

She was obviously trying to give us hints, and I was normally sensitive to such, but *living* and *dead* were only two categories. Perhaps if I divided one of the two ... I raised my hand.

"Ssster, Ssster." By third grade, the title of the nun had only one syllable, especially when pronounced by an eager hand-raiser.

"Yes, Edward?"

I knew I was reaching in my attempt, but I went ahead heartily. "The Church in Heaven, I mean the Catholics that have died and gone to Heaven, and the Church of Good Catholics on Earth, and the Church of people who aren't yet Catholic but are honorary Catholics. That's three."

This last category, I would realize later, was for my father and all the other good people whom I always felt belonged in Heaven anyway. Deep in the Catholic tradition was a dictum— "*Extra Ecclesiam nullam salus*"—"outside the Church there is no salvation." I would spend much of my youth trying to push that envelope. But that day there was a right answer to Sister's question, and my ruminations were not going to suffice.

"Well, Edward, that is three, and you've almost got the answer we're looking for. The Church in Heaven is certainly correct, and the Church of Good Catholics on Earth is also correct, although the Church on Earth includes both good Catholics—ones who go to Confession and Communion every week—and lapsed Catholics, who don't practice their faith at all. But there is also a place where Catholics are that isn't Heaven and isn't Hell ..." Sister drew three lines on the board. Next to the top one she wrote *Heaven*, next to the bottom one she wrote *Earth*, then turned to us. Many hands were up.

"Joseph?"

Joseph Tranchitella was the tallest in the class. He rose proudly and said "Limbo."

A few of the girls rolled their eyes. Everybody knew there were no Catholics in Limbo. Limbo was the place where unbaptized good people went—pagan babies who never had a chance to commit a sin, adult pagans who had led good lives, atheists of virtue, anyone who never heard of the Catholic church. Since all Catholics were baptized, none were in Limbo.

"Not exactly, Joseph, Limbo is the place where unbaptized people go. But that's a good try. No, this is a place where people are suffering for their sins." She paused, and then added, "But it isn't Hell."

Of course we knew it wasn't Hell because the space for the correct answer was not below Earth.

I looked out the window to think on a possibility Sister had just suggested. Were there Catholics in Hell? If there were, then they weren't part of the Church, I guess. Only those who had committed a mortal sin had gone to Hell. By turning their backs on God, had they excommunicated themselves? Adolf Hitler had been a Catholic, he had even been an altar boy, and he was certainly in Hell. It was true that we never prayed for the people in Hell. They were hopeless cases, I reminded myself.

As soon as the phrase *hopeless cases* entered my mind, it triggered a visual image of a small round gold medal that some of the women in our parish wore. Smaller than the Miraculous Medal and lacking that medal's oval shape, it held the picture of St. Jude—patron saint of hopeless cases. These icons were usually so small that the image of the apostle stamped on it was barely visible, but you could tell what it was from the shape and the color, and you could also tell something about the wearer— that he or she had some reality in his or her life that was a burden almost impossible to bear. St. Jude was the patron saint of last resort.

Part of the genius of the Catholic tradition, I would realize later on, is the large number of channels of communication with the Holy. God, of course, is the final judge and giver of grace, but between me and God there are many possibilities for intercession. First there is the Blessed Mother, the most influential. After all, she is the Mother of God, and even God has to listen to His Mother, as do we—both His and ours. But there is also a myriad of other figures to whom one can pray for blessings and favors—the patron saints. A visit to a religious articles shop in the 1950s would normally include perusing the medals case. Every profession was covered—policemen had St. Michael, actors had St. Genesius, travelers had St. Christopher (until his unfortunate official demise after Vatican II, which did not actually affect sales of that dashboard staple).

The message was that, if you were Catholic, you always had access to grace through intercession. Indeed, the inscription on the Miraculous Medal put it most succinctly: "O Mary, conceived without sin, pray for us who have recourse to thee." If one saint was not up to the job, there was always another possible focus for prayer.

The final refuge was St. Jude. I used to think that he was the patron saint of hopeless cases because his name was such a hopeless case—what tough luck to be an apostle with a name so easily confused with the one who betrayed Our Lord. Whenever I saw someone with a St. Jude medal, I would say a Hail Mary for their intention, whatever it might be.

And so that day I decided, looking out that window, to hook up the most hopeless cases in existence—the souls in Hell—with their patron saint, St. Jude. And why not, if we could pray for the souls in Purgatory to get out ... This thought brought me back to the question at hand—of course, the third part of the Church, that between Heaven and Earth, was the Church in Purgatory. My hand was up and straining to catch Sister's attention. But to no avail—I had already been called on once for this one, and Mary Watson was ahead of me.

"The souls in Purgatory?" she asked, shyly. Mary was one of those kids who knew a lot, but her shyness kept her from flaunting it in class.

"Very good, Mary, you're exactly right," said Sister as she placed the word next to the middle blank. "Now, children, I'm going to fill in these blanks and let you know the words that the Bishop might want to hear if he asks you a question on the night of your Confirmation."

Our hearts froze. The Bishop is going to ask us questions? This was the first most of us had heard of this. Those who had older brothers and sisters probably knew about it from watching their siblings' sacraments in former years, but I, being the oldest kid in my family, hadn't had that experience.

"The Bishop will ask several questions that night, and for the next few weeks we're going to be studying very hard to memorize the questions about Confirmation so we'll be ready."

Actually I enjoyed the extra pressure. By third grade I had become a kind of overachiever. I had won General Excellence and Religion awards in grades one and two, and thrived on the attention I got from knowing the answers. My father was always ready to help me with my homework, and it allowed us time together that we might not otherwise have. Showing a First or Second Honors card to my parents was one of the highlights of my youth.

The three levels of the Church were finally becoming clear to us as Sister wrote on the board: next to the word *Heaven*, "The Church Triumphant"; next to *Purgatory*, "The Church Suffering"; next to *Earth*, "The Church Militant."

"Now, children, why would we call the Church in Heaven 'the Church Triumphant'?" she asked.

Most of us raised our hands. It was an easy one compared to those leading up to it.

"Donna Kelly?"

Donna, the prettiest girl in our grade but not one to be called on much, rose and said triumphantly, "Because the ones in Heaven are the ones that blow trumpets." A few giggles punctuated the silence.

"Yes, Donna," replied the nun benignly, "it is true that we sometimes think of those in Heaven as blowing trumpets, or playing harps, and *triumphant* sounds like *trumpet,* but the word 'triumphant' means something a little different. Dennis?"

Dennis Coneen rose and said, "They are called triumphant because they have triumphed over evil and made it to Heaven." We all relaxed, the tension produced by the last answer relieved by the obviously correct one.

"Right. And the Church Suffering?" she said as she moved her pointer down to the middle line. This was easy. "Julie Vellutello?"

"Because the people in Purgatory are still suffering from the sins they committed on Earth and didn't have time to confess before they died," she said quickly and efficiently, her black ponytail bobbing as she sat down. I was glad I went to Confession every Saturday, so that if I died on any of the days in between, my time in Purgatory would be minimal.

"That's right," said Sister, moving her pointer down another notch to the line marked *Earth* and *Church Militant.* "Does anyone know what the word 'militant' means?"

No hands went up. We didn't, although I knew it had something to do with being alive.

"I'll give you a hint. Remember last week we talked about Confirmation as giving us the power to be somethings of Christ?"

I racked my brain. She was obviously trying to telegraph the answer. I thought, *Friends? Children?*—no, children of God, but not children of Christ, he was unmarried—*Helpers?* I thought back to the week before, sacking the file of my memory for clues. Nothing there.

"I'll give you another hint: 'The fighting Sixty-ninth.'"

A pause, and then it hit me. *Soldiers of Christ,* of course. My hand was up, straining for attention.

"Edward?"

"Soldiers of Christ. The Church Militant is the Soldiers of Christ on Earth," I said, looking around for adulation.

"Exactly. Now what are we on Earth fighting?" Many hands were up. "Michael Kane?"

"Commies. We are fighting against Communists all over the world, at home and abroad." He obviously remembered watching the McCarthy hearings on TV.

"It's true, Michael, Communism is a great threat to the Catholic church, but there are other forces closer to home. Like temptations to sin. Each of us individually is responsible for fighting the temptations we have in our own life, temptations to be selfish, to get angry, or to disobey our parents, things like that."

"Is it a sin to be angry at the Communists?" asked Michael, half-innocently, luring Sister into a trap of ideological debate, which she avoided by making a distinction we had heard about when a similar question had come up about Jesus' treatment of the money-changers in the Temple.

"It would be a sin to hate *them,* but it's not wrong to hate their sin. Just anger is all right." Then she quickly went on to the next question. The distinction between just and unjust anger would have to wait until I faced the Jesuits in college.

"Children, are these three groups"—pointing to the categories on the board—"three different churches, or all one Church?"

This was easy, it had the same structure as the question of three Persons and One God that we had learned a while back; all of us knew how St. Patrick had solved that one with the shamrock.

"Carolyn Reese?"

"Three churches in one Church," said Carolyn, paraphrasing the other solution about Persons and God.

"That's right, and how do the three connect? George Lotter?"

"I think I got it. We, the Church Militant, pray *to* the saints in Heaven, and they help us get the things we ask them to get for us, like grace and good marks in school. And we pray *for* the souls in Purgatory, so they can get to Heaven quicker." He paused. "But we sometimes ask the souls in Purgatory to help us get up on time."

I was impressed at George's answer, he had worked it out like an arithmetic question. Although Sister blanched slightly at the last insight, she did not deny it. Everyone knew that if you wanted to get up early, you could ask the souls in Purgatory to wake you. They had nothing better to do, I guess, it probably took their minds off their suffering a little. It had worked for me several times.

"Very good. Now here's another question, children, about the souls in Purgatory. How else can we shorten their stay there?"

This was an easy one, too: we could help them by "offering things up." This concept was at the root of Catholic experience in the 1950s. Later on I would learn of the Communist critique of this aspect of Catholicism, that it led to docility in the masses. But learning to offer things up was an integral part of our training, and a great technique for teaching us patience with discomfort, especially during Lent. It also helped us put up with injustice in our own lives. If we were wrongfully punished or otherwise offended, instead of fighting back or plotting revenge, the solution was to "offer it up." By putting up with pain on Earth we could somehow intercede for a soul in Purgatory and get them out even quicker. All Christians believe in the Communion of Saints, but for us kids, it was a tight and very functional reality.

My hand was up again, but she called on Bobby Gress.

"We can help them by offering up stuff, like when we have a toothache or are wrongly accused," he said.

"Right, Robert."

She reached under her bib and produced a small watch on a chain, looked at it, and concealed it again.

"Very well, children, it is almost time for recess. Look up at the right-hand corner of the board and copy down your homework assignments in Catechism for tonight. They include memorizing the seven gifts of the Holy Ghost. Tomorrow there might be a quiz in this, so good luck. Also, remember that tomorrow is First Friday. I'll see you all at Mass, and we'll have a late start for classes. Riders and bus children, bring breakfast to eat after Communion. Walkers, you may go home for breakfast, of course."

I shot a high sign back to my buddies, Walt Wiseley, Joe Wusinich, and Jackie Woulfe. Since my house was only three doors from the church property, they always came over to our house on First Fridays between Mass and class. It was my favorite kind of school day.

Having to memorize the catechism was no easy task, but I knew I could count on help from my dad. That night after dinner, we went over my homework together, him holding the catechism, me answering the questions.

"Name the seven gifts of the Holy Ghost," he began, after the table had been cleared.

"The seven gifts of the Holy Ghost are"—the catechism answers always repeated the question—"Wisdom, Knowledge, Fortitude, Temperance, Piety, Counsel, and Fear of the Lord," I rattled off, having learned not only the words, but the cadence they naturally embodied. That was one good thing about the catechism, whoever put it together usually ordered the answers in such a way that they would come off the tongue with rhythm.

"Very good, son, now do you know what these words mean?" he asked.

"Oh, we don't have to know the definitions yet, just the list," I shot back, actually not sure that we would ever have to know the meanings of the words—most of which I knew, anyway. "I am curious about one thing, though, what's the difference between Wisdom and Knowledge, do you think?"

"Well," he started, "Knowledge is the awareness of facts, of things that are true, and Wisdom is the ability to use those facts to lead a happy life."

"Oh," I said lamely. Wanting to continue the conversation, I said, "Can you give me an example?"

"Sure, I'll tell you a story about a boy who had knowledge but wasn't too wise.

"Once there was a boy who loved to play chicken with motorcycles in front of his house at night. He would stand out of sight until he saw a single headlight coming down the road, then he would jump out and stand there while the cycle zoomed by, just missing him. He was smart enough—he had the knowledge—to know how close he could stand without really getting hurt, but he didn't have the wisdom to know how foolish playing chicken really was.

"One night he was trying to show off in front of some friends. When he saw a single headlight, he took his position in the road. But by the time he realized it was a whole car with one headlight out, it was too late to move and he got mowed down. He never knew what hit him. His knowledge didn't help him at all."

I was surprised by the quickness of the ending, expecting the boy would learn a lesson in a lecture from his dad—my own favored mode of learning, not that it ever worked—but the story was over, the lesson learned, I supposed.

"Thanks, Dad," I said, dutifully resolving never to play chicken with motorcycles.

That night my sleep was filled with dreams of headlights and engines, and I got up late, almost too late for Mass, but I made it just in time to sit with my three friends. Afterwards the four of us came back to our house as planned. As we walked in the front door, the smell of French toast and slightly burnt hot chocolate filled our nostrils. I knew from the scent my mom had made the chocolate from scratch; instant cocoa doesn't burn, but real hot chocolate is impossible to make without burning a little. We flung our coats on the couch and went to the dining room table, where four glasses of orange juice were waiting. My family rarely ate dinner at this table, except on Sundays, and never breakfast, except on First Fridays. It made us feel very special, and a little grown up. We tried to act the part to some extent.

In came my mother with a big plate of French toast. "Good morning, boys," she said cheerily, beginning to place two slices on each plate.

"Good morning, Mrs. Stivender," answered three polite and happy voices, making my "Hi, Mom" seem almost impolite.

"And what was the gospel about this morning?"

"Oh, the regular," responded Joe, the smartest of the three. "Love your neighbor, be good like Jesus."

"And have Wisdom, Knowledge, Fortitude, Temperance, Piety, Counsel, and Fear of the Lord," I chimed in, being a smart kid and a showoff at the same time, my most developed skill.

"That's not the gospel, that's the catechism," chided Walt, proud that he had at least recognized it as such.

"It's in both," I protested, not actually knowing if this was the case. "You have the knowledge, but not the wisdom."

"Watch your temperance, Ed," said Jack, implicitly inviting the rest of us to join the game of using the words we had learned for homework the night before.

Joe picked up on it immediately. "I'll have another piece of piety."

We laughed, our mouths full, our minds racing to the next move, as we passed around the maple syrup and the cinnamon mix my mother had made by adding granulated sugar to powdered cinnamon.

Maple-syrupped French toast and orange juice mixed in the mouth made my fillings ache and my body shiver. It was grand.

"After school, ya wanna build a snow fortitude?" chipped in Walt. We grunted in derision, it was a little lame, that one.

"Hey, I heard your subscription to the Book of Knowledge was counseled," said Joe, proud to use two in one sentence.

"We're off to see the wisdom, the wonderful wisdom of Oz," added Jackie. We all booed at this one, it wasn't even close. We continued eating, semi-silently. Only Fear of the Lord was left. My imagination was working hard looking for a pun that wouldn't be blasphemous (or scatological, as my attempt at the wisdom one would have been).

Lord ... lid ... lewd ... lad ... loud—there it was, "Fear of the Loud" was the punch line, now all I needed was a setup. I could tell from the look on Wusinich's face that he was going through the same kind of drill, we were in a dead heat ... of course, Helen Keller. It would be a genre joke.

"What did Helen Keller never have?"

Realizing I had beaten him to the punch, Joe relaxed his frown and concentrated on my joke. "I give up," he finally admitted.

"Fear of the Loud!"

They all groaned in unison, loudly.

"Does anyone want seconds?" asked my mother from the door to the kitchen.

"No thank you," we all said, pretty full.

"Eat everything on your plate, now boys, remember the starving children in India."

"India?" questioned Jackie. "My dad always says they're in China."

"Starving children all over the world," said Joe.

"But none here at this table," said Walt. "Maybe I will have one more."

On the way back to school we played a quick game of SAC off the Masons' hill, and ran to the schoolyard just in time for the bell, then filed silently into the classroom for our Catechism class.

"Who can tell me the seven gifts of the Holy Ghost?"

Many hands went up, including Jackie Woulfe's. Sister was surprised, and couldn't resist the possibility of a correct answer from this less-than-serious student. "Jack Woulfe?"

My friend rose from his seat, and began the list, mumbling inaudible syllables to himself between correct answers. I realized that he was going over the foolishness at breakfast, mining the silliness for the knowledge it held. What wisdom, I thought to myself, remembering my father's lesson from the night before, proud of my ability to make the distinction.

"(Mumble, book of) knowledge, counsel, (piece of) piety, wisdom (of Oz), (watch your) temperance, (build a snow) fortitude, and (Helen Keller) fear of the loud"—he shot me a glance, then covered—"I mean Lord."

Some of the kids were laughing at this last part. Sister was not.

"Very good, Jack, I'm glad you've been studying."

At Stivender's dining room table, I thought to myself, proud of my friend and the educational value of our play.

"Now, children, the Bishop's visit is only three weeks away, so today we'll go down to the church and practice our procession and seating. Two lines at the front door, please— boys to the left, girls to the right. Quietly please, everybody make a sign of the cross on their lips."

We all did so, assuring ourselves and Sister that there would be no talking. The first graders used to zipper their lips, but by the time you were in third grade, you were expected to know the theological dimension of obedience, so we used the cross.

When we got down to the auditorium that served as our church as the parish collected money to build a real one, Sister maneuvered us into two lines down the center aisle that separated the two sets of rows of metal folding chairs, some so complex as to have kneelers attached to the back, and said something that would lead to ten minutes of necessary chaos.

"Now, children, line up by size." And the bustling began.

This was something that we had done two years before for May Procession, and just last year, for First Communion, but Mother Nature had had her way with us since then, and a few new kids had joined the class, so we had to start all over. That first year I had had the dubious honor of being in the front of the line but since then had grown a little. I knew I'd have a new position, but I didn't know how far back I'd be.

Lining up by size takes three people—two to stand back to back and a third to decide who is shorter. The noise in the room was growing, as squabbles were started and settled, Sister being the final arbiter of all disagreements. When it was all over, Sister went to the front of the line and did one last check by eye. She smiled. "Perfect."

"Now turn around, and process quietly to the vestibule. Remember who you are behind and who you are in front of. These will be your places when the Bishop comes."

In the vestibule, as the lines broke down so that we could all fit in the smaller space, chaos returned. Sister came back, her face reddening. "You are so many bold brazen articles," she yelled. "Did you forget the meaning of the word 'quietly'?"

This shut us up. We all froze as her color returned to normal. I was secretly glad she yelled at us then, actually, because at least once in a rehearsal of this sort the nun would have to get really mad, and the sooner the better, in my view. Things would run more smoothly now. I disliked chaos.

When she was finished yelling, we were all very quiet, looking down at our shoes, ashamed. I knew that somewhere in the room Jackie Woulfe was successfully stifling the laugh that could really get him in trouble. Sister was silent for longer than usual, glaring at us. I was relieved when she finally spoke.

"Now, students, when I make this sound"—a clicking sound filled the vestibule, we recognized it from our First Communion procession. In her hand she held a metal "cricket" like the ones you could buy at the five-and-ten, or which would come in the home version of "Jeopardy" years later, but the one Sister had was very big and made a very clear sound. "When I make that sound you are to start up the middle aisle, hands folded, with your partner, silently and slowly. When the first people get to the first pew"—folding chairs, but she still called it a pew—"they are to stop, and all of you are to stop in place. Do you understand this?"

"Yes, Sister," we all mumbled, afraid of the tremor still in her voice.

"Very well."

Click!

And we started up. The jumble of kids shuffled itself into a line amazingly well, and quietly too, some of us on tiptoes, myself included, wanting to maintain the silence fully. When the first two kids stopped, the rest of us stopped pretty much on cue, only one or two walking up the heels of the person in front of them.

"All right, now I am going to click the clicker again, and when I do you are all to genuflect on your right knee and stay down until you hear the second click, signaling you to rise."

Click! We all genuflected—and stayed down, some more successfully than others. There was some shuffling behind me and I imagined three or four kids had lost their balance, but I did not dare look back for Fear of the Nun. The noise subsided without a word from Sister.

Click!

And we all rose.

But apparently not completely together.

"We will try it again"—she paused, we knew what was coming—"until we get it right."

Click! Almost silence.

Click! We rose—almost together.

"We will try it again until we get it right if it takes us till dinnertime."

Click! Silence.

Click! We all rose.

And held our breath. It was good enough, I guess, because we did not have to do it again that day. I think Sister was using her wisdom; nothing would have been gained by continuing, tension is a terrible teacher, especially when assisted by hunger.

"Now, children, start entering the pews, five to a row, every other seat, leaving room for the sponsors who will sit next to you once you are seated ... slowly."

We took our places and stood in front of our seats waiting for another click to signal our sitting down.

Click! We sat.

Success. Collective sigh of relief.

I heard a familiar voice right behind me, whispering, "Fear of the Loud." Jackie Woulfe in the same seat, one row back, was testing the limits of behavior. I didn't dare respond, for fear we'd both get in trouble.

"So far, so good," said Sister, her voice relaxing. "At some point in the evening, the Bishop will come down from the altar and ask you the questions. Raise your hand only if you know the answer. We don't want to be embarrassed by a wrong answer. Some of the questions will be easy, some not so easy. If he calls on you, stand up and speak in a loud voice. Your parents want to hear your answer too."

Pressure, pressure.

"Any questions?"

Not a one.

"When it is time for the sacrament itself, the Bishop will come to the center aisle and stand there with his assistants. I will click the clicker, and you will all rise together, file out slowly to the center aisle, and up to the Bishop, your sponsor walking behind you. Does everyone understand?"

"Yes, Sister." In moments like this, we used both syllables.

She continued. "When you get up to the Bishop, with the sponsor behind you, he will ask you your Confirmation name. Say it in a loud voice. He will put some oil of chrism on your forehead while he says the name, and then he will tap you on the cheek. Why does he do that?"

Many hands went up.

"James Tracey?"

"So we can prove we're tough enough to be Soldiers of Christ, and worthy members of the Church Militant."

"Correct. Now here we go, pay attention, don't go too fast."

Click! We started up, Sister playing the Bishop. I proudly said "Patrick" when it was my turn. She just touched my cheek, it didn't hurt, like the Bishop's might, but I wouldn't flinch, not me, Soldier of Christ that I was.

We practiced all that day, missing recess as well as the threatened quiz. By the time the day was over we had it pretty well. Over the next three weeks, Sister drilled us with catechism questions until our heads spun with vocabulary and cadence.

I got new shoes in preparation for the event. The boys would wear their uniforms, though the girls were allowed to dress special. I was glad I was a guy.

The day of Confirmation finally came. Because the Bishop had to visit many parishes, some had their ceremonies right after school, but we had ours at night. After getting a haircut that afternoon, I was ready.

We gathered in our classroom at 6:30. There was hardly room for all of us and our sponsors, but we made do, jostling happily with our friends, the girls primping each other.

Click, click, click! When we quieted, Sister said, "It's time. Line up as you have practiced, and we'll begin our procession. Sponsors, hang back until the children are lined up in the church and then join them, sitting to their left if they are a boy and to their right if they are a girl, so you'll be behind them when you reach the Bishop."

These directions sounded very confusing to me, but the sponsors were all adults and seemed to understand.

I had always loved processions, and this one was going to be a great one. As we entered the church, the organ started playing and the choir started singing. I looked up to the altar and was amazed at how fancy it was, overflowing with flowers, every candle lit—quite a different look from all the rehearsals we had.

Below the altar, at the head of the main aisle, stood a man in a bright red satin robe with a gigantic golden hat, holding a big gold stick with a curlicue at the top, not unlike the staff of a shepherd in the nursery rhyme book at home, but much more ornate. On his right hand, I saw as we got closer, he wore a giant gold ring. We had learned that we would be expected to kiss this ring if we met him outside the Confirmation ceremony, but not during. I wondered about the germs involved in such a transaction. Did he wipe it off after each kiss?

When the first kids got to the first pew they stopped, and soon the entire line was still, no one's heels trampled.

Click! We genuflected.

Click! We stood. We were then joined by our sponsors and took our seats. Jackie Woulfe tapped three times on the back of my chair. I didn't look back but nodded slightly to let him know I knew he was there.

The first part of the Mass went smoothly. The most interesting thing was watching his assistant take off the Bishop's hat and put it back on, and care for his staff with a special cloth.

After the gospel it was time for the imposing figure to speak, in full regalia. His sermon was about Fighting Father Duffy. It gave the Bishop time to reminisce about growing up in New York and visiting Father Duffy's statue in Times Square.

"Actually, boys and girls, it's on a square all its own, called Duffy Square. It's a beautiful sight. At one end is Duffy, dressed in his trench coat, his battered breviary in his hand. He spent most of his time in the War in the trenches after all, caring for the men of the Fighting Sixty-ninth. And your pastor knows how tough war is." Here he glanced at Father Meyer, who had served as a chaplain in the Second World War, before accepting the pastorate at Holy Cross. The younger man nodded back sternly.

The Bishop continued, on a roll. "There's Duffy at one end, looking down Broadway at Times Square, and there at the other end of the triangle is a statue of a dancing man, George M. Cohan, the Yankee Doodle Dandy. And that statue of Duffy looking at the Yankee Doodle Dandy proves that you can be a good Catholic and a good American. The two go hand in hand. You can be a good Catholic *only* if you are a good American and are willing to give your life for your God and country, against the forces of godless Communism.

"You children are going to receive Confirmation in a minute. You've taken your basic training, your boot camp as it were, from the good Sisters, and you're like the squires of old, about to be dubbed full knights and take your place in the battle against the forces of evil. Are you ready?"

Was this one of the questions we had been warned about? Some kids nodded, not knowing if a response was expected of us. It was.

"Are you ready to become Soldiers of Christ?" he repeated in a louder voice.

"Yes," we all answered, some of us adding, "your excellency."

"Are you ready to take the blow on the cheek without flinching?"

"Yes!" A little louder this time. I wondered if it was going to hurt.

"Of course you are, and if a godless Communist soldier came in the back door right now and asked all the Catholics to line up and be shot, would you join me up here on the altar to die for your faith? Would you?"

There were a few enthusiastic responses. The tension in the room was growing. Supposedly he was only going to ask seven questions. Did these count?

"Of course you would. You are the Church Militant, and Fighting Father Duffy would be proud of you."

Not a sound in the church. He began moving toward us, his staff pounding each step as he descended the wooden stairs. It was ominous. *Here it comes,* I thought to myself.

"Now I've got some questions for you. Raise your hand if you know what my big hat is called."

Whew, I thought to myself. Sister had prepared us for this one.

He called on a girl, I couldn't tell who, couldn't hear her voice.

"That's right, a miter, and what's this?" he asked, holding up his staff.

He called on another girl, Marie Cathcart. "It's a crozier."

"Very good, now who can tell me what it represents?"

He called on someone behind me, but I didn't dare turn around. I didn't want to look at Jackie Woulfe, who was tapping his foot on the back of my chair.

"A shepherd's staff, your excellency." I recognized James Tracey, always a little too correct.

"Very good, and you even knew the proper form of address. You've had a good education, I can see that. Very good, Sister."

Sister nodded at this compliment, demurely.

"All right then, what do I remind you of?"

This stumped most of us for a minute. I sort of got where he was going with this, but not quite. Then I felt the tapping on the back of my chair intensify and heard the most articulate whisper.

"Big Bo Peep."

A sound escaped my lips. Not quite a laugh. Hoping it could have been mistaken for a cough, I coughed again. The sponsor on my right, Bill Schiochetti's older brother, had his head in his hand, I could feel his body shaking, but could hear no sound coming from him. I felt my face getting red. I tried not to breathe, for if I let any air go either way I would be a goner.

The Bishop was looking vaguely in my direction. I felt he was looking straight at me. I had to do something, to cover my convulsions. I reached into my pocket and pulled out a starched white handkerchief, buried my face in it, and finally breathed out, loudly, gasping for breath.

"Yes, young man," said the Bishop. I looked up, and thought he was pointing to me, but then I felt Jackie's hands on the back of my chair as he rose, covering my distress with his answer, letting me compose myself.

"The Good Shepherd, caring for his troops."

"Very good, young man, very creative thinking. Now, who can tell me what are the seven gifts of the Holy Ghost." He called on someone in the first row. The pressure was off.

The world began to return to normal. I caught my breath, no scandal occurred, several others had a chance to show off their catechism knowledge, and the Bishop said we were the sharpest class of confirmands he'd ever met. Which he told all the classes, I'm sure.

After the ceremony—I didn't crack up when the bishop struck my cheek, by the way, nor did I flinch—I caught up to Jackie Woulfe and punched him on the shoulder. He turned around and snickered.

"Gotcha, didn't I?" he gloated.

"Almost," I had to admit. "I think you've got the eighth gift of the Holy Ghost, though."

"What's that?"

"Timing."

"Nah, I got a better one. But I don't have it, you do."

"What?"

"Fear of the Laugh."

"Amen, Brother."

Sir Baseboard

*R*ow houses have been a Philadelphia tradition since William Penn designed them as an alternative to London's slums and firetraps. His great innovation was the placement of open parks every few blocks. These parks would make a city more livable and stop the sort of engulfing fire that had destroyed London in 1666. The result of his design is that the oldest section of Philadelphia is very orderly, blocks and blocks of houses set on streets that run straight, usually with an alley behind each row.

I grew up in a row house in the Philadelphia suburbs, in a place called Westbrook Park, whose developers attempted the row-house design on a hill that had once been a farm near Darby Creek. The curves of the hill did not allow for the straightness of the city townhouses, and the result was a kind of common space at the top of the hill, with row houses and alleys all around. Each of the row houses had a small yard behind it on the other side of the alley. Five back yards in a row would make a good field for touch football, if the neighbors didn't set up fences to ruin it. With the open part beyond our yards (abutted on the other side by a further series of row houses and yards) there was always good ground for playing War, or Cowboys and Indians, which we did with varying styles of sticks that could double for bows, spears, rifles, or tommy guns, depending on what game was being played.

I have a photograph of the core group of neighborhood boys sitting in winter on the field we played our games upon.

Robin Bates, who lived two doors down, was the biggest of the crew. Though a year younger than I, he was a formidable opponent in our football games. His younger brother Greg, who was able to push himself in with us older guys because of his agility and speed, was a natural athlete, often rigging home-made high-jump apparatuses and using bamboo poles to vault them.

Bobby Forbes, my next-door neighbor, was meatier than the rest of us—and therefore a little slower—but worth his weight when push came to shove. His younger brother, Gary, the youngest kid in the group, was scrappy and always ready for adventure.

Michael Hall, our neighbor on the other side, was about my size, and also a Catholic, a year behind me at Holy Cross Elementary School.

Jimmy Smith, in the house on the other side of the Bateses, was the most protected of us kids. He wasn't always allowed to play with us, and when he did, he would be called in for supper by his mother clapping her hands at the window. This impersonal gesture seemed to be some subtle form of abuse, and I always felt sorry for him. On the other hand, being an only child, he had the most toys, in the best shape.

Michael Kanouse rounded out the gang. He was a "public," like most of the other kids, going by bus to the Primos, the public elementary school. He was a great theoretician, sharp when it came to football or stone-throwing strategy.

Because of the numerous construction sites nearby, we had access to unlimited amounts of scrap wood for such exercises. One day I found a three-foot piece of molding—the kind used to cover the space between floor and baseboard—and immediately recognized the stick's suitability for sword play. Its superiority derived from its being rounded on one side so that you could pull it easily out of your belt loop and brandish it in the air for a charge on the enemy. As I mastered various maneuvers with the sword, I earned the nickname—more nearly a character—of Sir Baseboard.

The weapon did have one limitation. The sticks my comrades all had were being used for guns—not belt-looped, not brandished, but with the capacity to kill the enemy at a distance (say, a back yard away). Although this would seem a problem, it was actually an advantage because it meant that (especially if you were leading the charge) you could be the first to fall in battle—which of course was the best part of playing War anyway—throwing up the hands, crying out, "I'm shot, men, carry on without me." Pretending to die was always the most fun.

Our game was influenced by the movies we saw. Audie Murphy gave us a repertoire of facial expressions to copy; the ethnic stars that graced all the World War II movies gave us their inter-dialect banter as they prepared for battle; we learned how to walk with a wounded leg, and so forth. When we saw *The Sands of Iwo Jima*, we were impressed by a scene near the end, when a Japanese sniper popped out of a metal tube to shoot John Wayne. In short order, we added a trash can to house a sniper on our battlefield.

When we started getting bikes, however, the war game changed. At first we forgot all about it as our horizons broadened to include the network of alleys we could ride at top speed, scaring the kids on blocks that were too far away for our games of Army but not too far to explore. Bikes and Army didn't mix well for another reason—you really couldn't die well off a bike without getting yourself or your bike broken or scraped. But you could do reconnaissance—ride around the alleys and look at the fortifications and playing fields of the enemy, which now included (in our imaginations) players we didn't really know well—other groups of kids, with their own Army game formats and hiding places. Some of these kids we knew from school but never hung out with in the afternoons because they lived out of earshot of our parents' call.

One particular group of boys lived over the back-yard hill who were a little older than us, and perhaps a little tougher. Their leader, Ricky Siddons, had armpit hair by the time he was in Webelos, that transition between Cub and Boy Scouts.

One August afternoon after my third-grade year, our crew decided to take a ride through their alleys. They were playing basketball behind Siddons' house. One of their neighbors was washing his car, making a delicious puddle the whole length of the alley. As we came around the corner and saw the situation, I drew my sword. (Whereas guns on bikeback were pretty useless, the baseboard sword could be used to better advantage in this calvary charge than on the battlefield, even though it did not facilitate dramatic death.)

"Full splash ahead!" I shouted, and we drove through their game in a surprise attack, splashing Ricky and the other players as we rode, our fenders protecting us in ways that today's fancy bikes would not. Their pant legs wet, their pride wounded, they saw the challenge and ran for their bikes to pursue us.

The alleys were connected in a large circle so that we could return to base without turning around and facing our pursuers, who were now coming on fast.

Gregory Bates was getting nervous. "Whose idea was that?"

Instead of taking the blame, I countered, "Knock it off, Greg, they won't catch us, we'll go in Forbeses' garage"— which, luckily, was open.

When the five of us were inside, Bobby Forbes pulled the door down, its rollers squeaking, and we watched Ricky's gang ride by in a quandary, looking for their lost quarry, as we gazed on through the cracks in the garage door.

They stopped their bikes, and knowing we lived somewhere around there, Ricky shouted, "Springfield Road Gang, the Ricky Gang hereby challenges you to a rock-throwing fight on Saturday, over the common ground, at twelve noon. Be there or be fairies." Then they got on their bikes and rode off.

"Are they gone?" came a voice from behind a stack of tires.

"They're gone, for now," said Michael Hall, "but they might be back."

"Then I'm staying here."

"Don't worry," said Bobby Forbes, raising the door and letting in the afternoon light on a scared Jimmy Smith, face marred with tire dirt, "they won't be back till Saturday."

"That's tomorrow," said Jimmy. "I think I'll be sick tomorrow."

"Sick on Saturday?" I scoffed. "Now there's a great way out, you'll blow the whole day sitting in your bedroom."

"Yeah," he sniffled, "but at least I can watch the rock fight out my window."

Nothing I could say would change his mind. He would have a great view, and he wasn't going to be much help in the battle anyway.

"We better start getting some rocks and stones, we can hide them in the back of our yard until tomorrow," said Robin Bates, taking charge.

"You really want to fight these guys?" I asked, silently calculating our chances, the moment of bravado giving way to rational thought. As I saw it, the odds were not good. The kids in the Ricky Gang were bigger, tougher, and probably had better rocks and throwing arms. Besides, there were more of them ... My mind was producing and repeating images of fear faster than I could think. I called on my secret Catholic weapon—the Hail Mary.

Even today, TV sports announcers on Saturday afternoon football games use the phrase "Hail Mary Play" to refer to a long pass downfield that has little scientific chance of being caught successfully but is ostensibly accompanied by the prayer of the quarterback for success. This short prayer, not quite short enough to be an ejaculation like "Jesus Mary and Joseph" but shorter than the Our Father, includes the Angel Gabriel's address to Mary at the Annunciation, as well as her cousin Elizabeth's greeting at the Visitation.

Hail Mary, full of grace, the Lord is with thee. Blessed art thou amongst women and blessed is the fruit of thy womb, Jesus. Holy Mary, mother of God, pray for us sinners now and at the hour of our death. Amen. It is a wonderful way for a Catholic kid in trouble to clear his mind and calm down his system. It worked for me. It always has. It still does. It has to do with breathing at the very least, and with supernatural grace at the very most.

As I calmed down and my mind cleared, I was able to focus on my friend's answer, which had to do with pride of the neighborhood and our group of kids: "We're a team, ain't we?"

"*Ain't* ain't in the dictionary," corrected Jimmy Smith, now fully recovered from his hiding, face washed with the water hose and dried with a rag.

"Yeah, we're a team all right, but they're a *gang*. Just look at their name—the *Ricky Gang*," Michael Hall observed, suggesting a distinction that only a Catholic education could have produced. Even today, it's not easy to tell the difference between a neighborhood club and a gang.

I'm not sure if the name "Ricky Gang" came from them or us originally. We never thought of ourselves as the "Springfield Road Gang," although we did live on Springfield Road and riding bikes to splash another group of kids might be considered gang-like.

Trying to lighten up the situation, I started to sing a song from a popular television show hosted by Andy Devine, better known as Wild Bill Hickok's sidekick, Jingles:

I've got a gang
You've got a gang
Everybody's gotta have a gang
But the bestest gang in the whole wide world
is good old Andy's Gang!

We all sang the last line together, it lifted our spirits somewhat.

"Yeah," said Jimmy, breaking our spell, "where's Andy when we need him?"

"Where's Wild Bill?" I joined in.

"Well, I'm going over to the field to get some stones," said Robin Bates, whipping his invisible horse as he ran down the alley and across the street to the vacant lot we used as a fort, where there were many good stones of various sizes.

"Hey, Wild Bill!" I cried out in a cracking voice like Andy Devine's at the opening of the cowboy series. "Wait for me!"

In an hour there was a pile of rocks, mostly fieldstone, in the back yard, in sight of where the Ricky Gang would appear at noon the next day. We discussed strategy until our mothers simultaneously appeared at our respective kitchen windows to call us in to supper.

Friday night dinner in my Catholic mother's household was always meatless and consisted of three choices: macaroni and cheese, fish sticks, or, on special occasions, pizza from the hoagie shop. That night we had fish sticks and french fries, eating in the living room while my three sisters and I watched "Riders in the Sky," a Western TV serial.

After dinner, I was allowed to go to Bateses', two doors down, to watch Friday night television. Friday was always the best night for us kids in those days. Warner Brothers produced a series of action shows, beginning with "Jim Bowie" ("His blade was tempered and so was he / Indestructible steel was he") and ending with "77 Sunset Strip" *(snap, snap).* As we sat and watched and drank soda served to us by Robin and Greg's mother, Miriam, we discussed the plan for the next day.

"If only we had Bowie knives," said Greg, as we watched the hero use his knife to solve all kinds of problems—from scaling walls to skinning dinner to catching outlaws—"or some secret weapon."

"Yeah," we all agreed.

"Even a comb like Kookie"—the star valet parking attendant of "77 Sunset Strip"—said Jimmy Smith.

"What good would a comb do?" I asked.

"We could flick the hair grease from it and blind the Ricky Gang," retorted my friend.

"Yeah, if only we had some secret weapon ... besides rocks and stones," dreamed Greg.

"Or sticks that were really magic."

"Like Sir Baseboard's?" kidded Mike.

On the screen a white tornado solved a housewife's cleaning problem with just such magic. I picked up a storybook from the magazine rack and opened it to a story about a lonely girl who had no friends because she was sickly and her mother wouldn't let her out of her third-floor bedroom. She spent all of her time at her window.

"Hey, Jimmy," I chided, "here's a story about a girl who watches everything from her window because she's sick, or pretending to be sick."

"Let me see that," said my friend, trying to see if my chiding had basis in literary fact. I handed the book over to him so he could see the picture of the girl looking sadly out the window. In the corner of the picture, a boy walked below, holding a stick of some kind to his mouth.

"What's that kid doing below the window?" asked Greg.

"Having a rock fight with the Ricky Gang?" I kidded, needing Jimmy's solidarity for the next day.

"No, I think it's a peashooter. Hold on." He skimmed the story quickly, then read aloud: "And the pea that the boy shot up to her window to get her attention that day lodged in a bit of dust by the windowsill and grew into a beautiful flowering vine that grew around the window and cheered the girl so much that she got well and was allowed to go outdoors, and was never sick again, the end."

"Does she marry the kid?" I asked.

"It doesn't say, but that's it. Our secret weapon."

"Love? Hey Ricky Gang, come here, we want to kiss you…" We began to move toward him, making kissing sounds, oblivious to the theological implications of potential peacemaking.

"No, get offa me, not love! Peashooters!"

The next morning we took parts of our allowances and headed to the row of shops at the top of the hill on Springfield Road. There was a bakery (Yeager's), a hoagie shop, a one-hour martinizing dry cleaner, two drugstores—one with a fountain that served chocolate snowballs (no kidding, pure chocolate on ice), the other with a display rack of *Classics Illustrated* comic books—a jewelry store, two barbershops, a shoe store, a five-and-ten, a hardware store, a dance studio, two grocery stores, and finally, a gift shop.

It was called Westbrook Park Gift Shop, and it was run by two women we assumed were sisters. They sat in the back where they would wrap gifts for free, but whenever they saw us coming they would meet us in front to lead us to the toy section and away from the china and porcelain stuff that we would only look at around Mother's Day. The rest of the time our goal was the shelves in the back—shelves that held boys' treasures, much of which would end up in our teachers' desks as contraband commandeered in the schoolyard. There were slingshots with real leather pouches, pimple balls, pink balls, toy soldiers, cowboys, Indians, and calvary, bullroarers (streamers on a string with a rubber band on a card contraption that sang as you whipped it around your head), jacks (for your sister's birthday), water pistols (little and big), Duncan yo-yo's—with a stripe for thirty-nine cents, with inlaid jewels and steel axles for ninety-nine cents—cap guns and caps, and rockets with metal firing pins that detonated the inserted caps on contact with the ground. There were all kinds of good things, including plastic peashooters for five cents and little bags of perfectly round and well-fitting peas for the same price.

The six of us (for Jimmy was in fact nowhere to be found) burst through the door and were at the shelves in the back before either sister could greet us.

"We're here for peashooters and peas, we don't need any help." The reason this stuff was in the back was so that they could watch us as we browsed. Never did we browse without an imposing presence hovering over us. This time it was the bigger sister's turn.

"There are two kinds, we just got the new kind in," she said, pointing to a new box. I reached in and pulled out a metal tube with a wooden mouthpiece. I wondered how the wood would taste, though I didn't experiment—equally nervous about germs and our hosts' response to such an attempt.

"How much?"

"The new ones are ten cents, the others are still a nickel."

"And the bags of peas?"

"Still five cents."

"Got any bigger bags than those? We may need a lot."

"That's the only size we have. You can buy dried peas at the supermarket, though."

"No, we tried that," piped up Greg, "they were too small."

"And wrinkled," added his brother. The little bag did hold big peas. "We'll take one of each."

"That'll be sixty cents."

We each gave her a dime and ran out the door back home to prepare for the noontime confrontation. The plan we devised would place two of us in the bushes beside their base of operation and where we could get them without being seen. There was a hole in the fence, right in back of our house, through which we could sneak around behind enemy lines and take up our position.

"I'll volunteer," I said, grasping the hilt of my now useless but decoratively symbolic baseboard sword, which I had taped with silver duct tape so anyone could tell it wasn't just a stick.

"Anybody else?" asked Robin, eyeing the group. There were six of us in all. Jimmy watched from his window. One of the non-volunteers had thrown him a shooter with peas to make him feel part of it, but his mother had confiscated the weapon and made him close the window. He gave the thumbs-up sign whenever we looked up.

"I'll go alone," I said. "It'll be better in case they discover us ... I mean me."

"Whatever you do, don't get captured," said Bobby Forbes. "They'll throw you in with the boxer."

My heart missed a beat at the thought of the Siddons' big dog, King, which was kept in their fenced-in yard. All the Ricky Gang kids had fences in their smaller yards, but we didn't and we felt lucky. Perhaps that was the basis of the conflict, militarily—the have-yards-for-ball and the have-nots.

Spending time in the doghouse was something I knew about from a wall hanging in our kitchen, a souvenir from South Carolina. It had pegs to hang the names of people in the family, and when someone was in trouble, he or she was put "in the doghouse." But the doghouse in the Siddons' back yard was less figurative and probably smelled bad. I had never been close enough to find out.

"Do you have your cyanide pill?" asked Robin.

"Very funny," I said as I squeezed through the hole in the fence. I crept around to my position, almost out of sight from anybody in the area but with a view of the other gang's headquarters. I tried a few shots and saw that my range was pretty good. I shot a couple of roofers and one pea went so high it disappeared. I gave my friends the high sign as they stood next to their individual rock piles.

And then we heard them coming—the Ricky Gang. They were singing the theme song from a TV show: "Robin Hood, Robin Hood / Riding through the glen." I looked through the bushes and saw first the ten of them, and then the large bags of rocks they carried. Somebody had even borrowed a paper route bag from an older brother. They took their positions and put the bags down. Each took a rock out of the bag and stood there, tossing the stones lightly and catching them in their hands. Who would cast the first stone?

It was Ricky, their leader. Soon the sky was filled with rocks, some aimed well, some not aimed at all. One rustled the bushes near my position. I held my fire, waiting until they were low on ammo. This turned out to take longer than I hoped, since in rock war there is a constant supply thanks to the reusability of the enemies' weapons. Eventually, though, my friends began to retreat, returning fewer and fewer rocks. No one had been hit on bare skin yet, but our younger boys had panicked and run into the house, and the others were being forced back to the alley. The Ricky Gang was beginning to advance when I finally opened fire.

I emptied an entire bag into my mouth and shot the peas one by one, my aim getting better with each shot, easier as there were fewer peas in my mouth to block the process. Most of mine were lower body shots, falling against denim and not felt by the victims, who were still advancing toward my friends and nearing the hole in the fence.

I re-beaned and aimed higher. Three shots in a row found the necks of Ricky and two of his henchmen. They looked around wildly for the source of the pain, expecting to see one of us on the adjacent alley on the other side of the bush that was my pillbox. I held still as they gazed over, under, around, and through me in my bush, but saw nothing. They refocused on the battle in front, nearing the hole in the fence and the underground path to my position. A few more steps, and they'd be on top of me.

Knowing the jig was up and fantasizing that I would save my friends, I jumped out of the bush and began firing full force at the gang, giving my friends time to escape into their houses and me the chance to play the foolish hero. I was tackled from behind by reinforcements, disarmed of my peashooter, and encircled by the enemy. Clothesline was produced and I found myself being marched down the alley towards a POW camp guarded by a large boxer named King.

The dog was barking loudly, though not viciously, as we approached the gate. I saw he was chained up to a steel peg driven into the ground next to his doghouse. It occurred to me that King might be in the doghouse himself, chained to prevent him from tunneling under the fence to his neighbors' yards.

I was pushed into the yard. I backed away from King, who was growling but still chained, thank goodness.

"All right," said Ricky. "Jim, ask the prisoner his name."

"What is your name?" asked the biggest kid, though not the smartest, his face inches from my own.

"My name is Sir Baseboard, and my serial number is 394582."

Ring, ring! The sound came over the housetops from the street in front—the Good Humor Man!

"Jim, you guard the prisoner. Everybody else, deploy for ice cream."

"Hey bring me somethin', will you?" called Jim.

"Sure, sure," the other boys called over their shoulders as they disappeared around the front. I was saved, as it were, by the bell—at least for the moment.

"They won't, you know," I said to Jim, trying not to cry. The dog was straining to break his chain—with the goal of doing more than sniffing my crotch, I imagined. "They won't buy you ice cream." This was a technique I had seen in a John Wayne movie, trying to drive a wedge between friends on the other side.

"Will, too."

"Will not." Over his shoulder I could see a strange sight, a boy on a bike, holding an empty bike by its handle—my bike. It was Michael Kanouse, my rescuer!

"Will, too."

"Go see for yourself," I taunted, praying he would.

"Nice try, prisoner," said the big kid with only a flicker of doubt on his face. "I'll go around front and you'll escape. Forget it."

"Not very likely, not with my hands tied and all my friends ditching me ..."

I emphasized the word *ditching* to show the supposed hopelessness of my situation and subliminally suggesting what could happen to him. The fear of being ditched, especially for a slightly goofy big kid that can't run as fast as the others, must be the primary motivation for many of the rituals of male society, the reason for ultrapatriotism and fraternity abuse.

"... And this vicious dog right here," I continued. "No, I'll be here for a while until my mother calls the cops."

He wasn't ready for this remark. He knitted his brow for a second. If the cops came right then, he would be blamed for the whole kidnapping, and then he'd really be in trouble, and the gang—with or without his ice cream—would certainly scatter.

And then my *coup de grâce,* delivered innocently: "Do you think they'll bring *me* back an ice cream?"

"I'll go find out," he said, turning quickly and moving in the direction of the ice cream bells. He wheeled about, now completely confused: "What flavor ..." He checked himself, said, "Stay right there," and disappeared around the front of the house.

Michael rode up, but the gate was locked and I couldn't climb over it with my hands tied.

"Come on, Ed. Let's get going."

"I can't climb tied up."

"Turn around, I'll untie you." His arms just reached over the fence.

As I turned I faced King. There was foam on his teeth. I was trying not to cry when I saw the hole the dog had made through the fence. Mike was getting nowhere with the knots.

"Mike, forget it, I'll go through the hole over there." I made my way cautiously around King, lay down, and started sidling through, with the dog inches from my face. Suddenly I was stuck. I thought King had a hold on me, and my heart stopped. Then I realized the rope was caught on the fence's bottom chain links.

Then I remembered something my uncle had told me about Houdini. My Uncle Ed, married to my Aunt Fran, taught me to play chess and knew a lot about extraordinary people and things. He said that Houdini had done all his escapes by breathing out and wriggling like a snake. Choking out a sob at this point went a long way toward emptying my chest, and wriggling was no problem, as panic was setting in.

I got out just as I heard a chain snap. A few seconds later, King was through the escape hole and on my side of the fence with my pant cuff in his mouth, growling. Mike was working on the knots that held my hands behind me. When I was free, I took my baseboard sword out of my belt loop and waved it in front of King's eyes. He let go of my pants and, as a diversionary tactic, I threw the stick a few feet away. The dog went for it, and Mike and I jumped on our bikes and escaped, the voices of the returning ice-cream eaters vainly sounding the alarm. When they saw King at large, they ran after him. They were too busy getting the dog back inside his kennel to worry about me.

We returned to our gang, holed up in Bateses' basement. Greg was holding ice in a cloth to a cut on his shoulder. We all had Kool-Aid, thanks to their sister Cynthia, and spent the rest of the day extolling our own bravery, my meeting with King and the big kid growing in detail and bravado with each telling. Mike Kanouse, however, was named M.V.P. for the day.

It was our last rock fight. That summer, when my friends and I attended Boy Scout camp, we were taken aback to find the Ricky Gang—without King—in attendance. But there we had a common goal—survival—and we teamed up against the wilderness and conveniently forgot the struggle of the rock war.

I never did get my sword back. It wouldn't have been any good after King was through with it, all slobbery and all. But I still have the nickname, in the alleys of my mind.

The Skateboard

I never really got the knack of roller skating, but I was always fascinated by the hardware. In my tradition (by which I mean Caucasian-Suburban-American of the mid-twentieth century), girls were not trained in the use of hand tools, usually had nothing to do with them. The notable exception was the skate key: it was a tool that girls were expected to know how to use. My sisters were very good at it. When a skate came loose, they would stop, and with a flick of the wrist on their upturned sole, they were off and rolling. It was a long time before I even knew what was going on in this operation.

The key itself had a wide butterfly-shaped top and a square wrench head. It was a real machine, I would learn later on in high school, a way to make metal move in a way that pinched the toes of the shoes, lending a snug fit to the feet so the skates wouldn't come off in transit. The key also allowed the length of the skate to be changed, in case the wearer was growing or kind enough to lend her skates to a bigger-footed person, like her older brother. Which never happened in my family.

I had no interest in skating, thank you, not since a bad fall I enjoyed before I was old enough to go to school. My original skates, the ones I had fallen in, had laces, not a mechanism that required a key, so I never learned how to use the key.

Although I had no use for skates per se, old skates were another issue entirely. With one old skate—plus a two-by-four, an orange crate, a couple of sticks, some nails, and a little paint—you could have an extraordinary vehicle: an orange-crate scooter.

I think my neighborhood gang first got into this mode of · downhill transportation when it became clear that none of our dads had the tools, the know-how, or the inclination to help us make a full-size soapbox derby car, which was the next logical step after the miniature soapbox race cars we carved as a badge requirement for Scouts. Orange-crate scooters were a compromise.

The odd thing about my interest in a homemade downhill vehicle was, I already had a scooter—a real good one, strong metal painted red, with grooved tracks for my right foot, a kind of bumper in the front, real rubber wheels, and rubber handlebar covers complete with streamers. The braking mechanism even allowed you to skid and make sliding gravel stops at the bottom of the hills that framed our block of row houses—two hills, which we, in a great burst of creativity, called "the big hill" and "the little hill."

They were the same hill topographically, but on it were laid two concrete alleys at either end of the one that ran directly behind our double block of fifteen houses. The height and pitch of the two hills were different, however, thanks to the way the natural contours of the farmland, on which the Westbrook Park row houses were built, rolled. The nice thing about the big hill was that it had an extra extension, a second slope after leveling off. We sometimes called this "the little little hill." Few cars used the alleys so it was possible for us kids to go down them with a degree of safety.

We rode these hills with several different conveyances: sleds in the winter (my family had the biggest sled of anyone in the neighborhood—eight feet long, an American Flyer), tricycles (I still have a scar on my forehead from my trips down the big hill and little little hill at the bottom of which there was a large crack in the concrete which I rarely avoided—with the same consequence each time), the aforementioned scooter, my Radio Flyer wagon (seats three, but dangerous turning while in the front seat).

Late one June morning of my fourth-grade summer, when school had been out long enough for us to start to be bored and blasé about the whole summer vacation experience, I was browsing through my July issue of *Boys' Life* reading the cartoons and jokes in the centerfold. I flipped the page and saw some kids whizzing down a hill on gaily painted orange-crate scooters. The accompanying article contained easy building instructions. This was just the thing to get our summer going again.

I ran out back and set up the call to my friends. One of the advantages of row houses is that you can call up to the windows of several friends at once while standing in the same spot.

"*Ee-yah-kee*," I called up, scanning the kitchen windows of all four houses that held my tribe. "Hey, youse guys, I got a great idea for an adventure."

Three burr-cut heads—Robin Bates, Michael Hall, and Bobby Forbes—appeared behind window screens.

"Ee-yah-kee, Steamboat," responded Robin Bates, using the nickname I had gotten playing touch football the winter before. "What's all the racket?"

"Hey, youse guys, look at this," I shouted, holding up the new *Boys' Life* (not without a little pride: I was the only kid on my block who received it, being the only Boy Scout that really went to meetings and the one with a wonderful godmother, my

Aunt Fran, who subsidized my subscription). Of course, no one could see the pictures clearly from that distance, so we decided to have a meeting in the Bateses' basement.

Of all the basements on the block, I liked the Bateses' best. The Forbeses had a tremendous workshop in theirs, but that didn't leave much room to have a meeting. The Halls' basement was fairly interesting, but they had a lot of kids, so there was always stuff all around. Our basement I knew too well, and it was my job to keep it clean, so that was no fun. The Bateses' basement had the most room, and the neatest smell. It was tiled and partially finished, and it smelled a little like my grandmother's house. Also, Mrs. Bates, the prettiest mom on the block, brought us Kool-Aid without even asking. So we met there.

Soon our gang of four—plus Robin's younger brother Greg—had gathered. I opened my magazine triumphantly and laid it before them. "Gentlemen," I said, "our summer just got exciting."

Greg said, "We could build one of those, easy."

Bobby Forbes said, "Yeah, if we had the crates, and the wood ..."

"And the skates," added Michael Hall.

Robin began to sing:

To build it we could
If we only had the wood
If we only had the crates
If we only had the skates.

Feeling that the project was not garnering the seriousness of tone necessary to get started, I said, "Crates we can get at Burrell's or Sloan's (the two grocery stores up the street) ..."

"Or from the huckster," added Mike, referring to the Italian man who drove his wood-panelled, open-back station wagon through the alleys just before suppertime every night.

"My dad's got two-by-fours in the garage, and we can use his saw and hammer," Bobby Forbes chimed in.

"We got nails," I added. My dad wasn't much of a handyman, but there were all kinds of nails in a discarded dresser in our garage.

"Big deal, nails," chided Greg.

"More than you got," I shot back.

"Nuh-unh," Greg responded, "we got paints ... yeah, and hammers."

He had me there, I had to admit, I could never find our hammer. I imagined it was somewhere in the chaos of the basement that I was supposed to be in charge of cleaning.

"Anybody got skates?" Robin's question stopped our conversation.

"I'm pretty sure I got my old ones, from when I was a kid," I offered, my mind's eye going to the big box under the cellar stairs, full of old shoes, ice skates, and other assorted footwear, as well as old Sears catalogs and *Life* magazines. The roller skates should be in good shape, since I had only used them once; with a little oil ...

"We only need three pairs for the six of us," said Bobby Forbes, pointing to the picture on the page, and a diagram showing how to take one skate apart for two front and two back wheels for each scooter.

"My sister just got new skates, I'll bet she'd give us her old ones," chimed in Michael Hall.

"If you ask real real real nice," Robin taunted.

"I think I got some old skates somewhere in my dad's garage," said Bobby Forbes. "I'll go look."

"OK," said I, trying to regain control of the group as ringleader—after all, it was my idea, my *Boys' Life*—"let's meet behind my house with all the supplies in a half hour, and we'll take it from there."

Just then Mrs. Bates came down the stairs with grape Kool-Aid and doughnuts she had bought from the Bond Bread man. We ate quickly and then split up to get to work.

Our basement was pretty dark normally, and under the stairs it was particularly so. I switched on the light above the sink near the wringer washer, drew back the curtain sheet that acted as a door to the storage area, and tacked it up to use the available light. There it all was, in a jumble. I threw myself into the search with gusto. The first thing I came upon was a back issue of *Life* magazine. I laid it carefully aside for later perusal, and started lifting items aside: several pairs of ice skates that must have belonged to my mother when she was a kid, some volumes of an encyclopedia, some old clothes, a worn-out portable vacuum cleaner. I kept digging until my hand felt something round and rough attached to something metallic. Then I felt a shoelace— my old skate, one of them at least. The other one came easily to my hand, now that I knew the general area of the box that held them.

There was a bit of rust on the tops of the skates, but the wheels were in pretty good shape, and they did come apart into two pieces like I hoped. After feeling around for the hammer, I stuffed all the things I had strewn about in my search back into the box and went out to the garage to find the nails.

The garage was one of my favorite places in the world. It took up about half the space of the ground floor of the house, and would have been a good place to keep our car, but my father insisted on keeping it out front—to show it off, I think, it was a Plymouth Cedarwood with hydromatic clutch—so the garage was available to us kids for rainy day play and for the shows we regularly produced. Putting on these shows was the only time my sisters and I really played together. We would string up a tablecloth curtain, borrow chairs from upstairs, dig into our parent's cedar chest for costuming pieces, and really go to town, presenting versions of fairy tales or stories we made up on our own, sometimes with puppets. My sister Nancy, just one year younger, would be the producer as well as the queen, making sure everything was just so, props and all. The one consistent thing in the presentations was our younger sister Mary's rendition of a song that didn't make sense until she delivered the climactic last line—"All day!"—with her arms raised like a real professional. Our youngest sister, Karen, was typecast as the baby, since she was one, at least during the time I was active in the garage theater.

During times when our theater wasn't having a show, the garage was a perfect fort for me. I had claimed it by painting mysterious runes and symbols on the cement walls. Under the runes was the chest which I hoped held the nails. The dresser itself was a beautiful ornate piece that had belonged to my mother's parents. She and my father had taken it in their move to Westbrook Park, in my first year of life, but when they finally got their own bedroom set, the ornate piece was banished to the garage to become a holding place for what few tools and supplies my father had.

I opened the top drawer quickly, revealing to the dim light the boxes of nails, some small, some large. There was a whole box of what my father called sixteen-penny nails, exactly what I was looking for, just perfect for affixing roller skates to two-by-fours. I opened another drawer, hoping against hope, and let out an almost silent cheer—there was the elusive hammer.

I reached into the cupboard at the bottom of the dresser for the can of oil I would use to lubricate the skates. When I pulled it out, I spilled some of the oil on the cement floor, where it joined the other stains. I looked behind the dresser and in all the crannies of the garage hoping to find a two-by-four, or something suitable, but could find none. What I did find, however, were several unused paint stirrers, flat contoured pieces of wood just a little longer than a ruler. These would be perfect for the handlebars.

I also found a bucket of wall paint, about three-quarters full. Only a few more things and I'd be ready—some empty tin cans for "headlights," some red reflectors for safety lights, and streamers for the handlebars. I took the streamers off my old scooter, ran upstairs to search through the trash for the cans, trying to remember if we had had peas recently, since two LeSeuer cans would be perfect. I found nothing suitable in the trash but did spy two full cans in the cupboard. I called upstairs to my mother.

"Mom, can we have peas tonight?"

A pause, and then she came to the top of the stairs with a puzzled look. "I suppose we can, although this is the first time you've asked for them that I can remember. What's going on?"

"Oh, nothin', just feel like peas, I guess."

"OK, then we'll have peas."

"Two cans worth?"

"That's a lot of peas, I usually open one can when we have potatoes ..."

"I'll eat them all, I promise."

"All right then, two cans." She turned to go back to her work.

I waited a moment before I got to the point. "Can I open the peas now and put them in the saucepan with a plate over it?

I'll put them in the refrigerator to keep them fresh till dinner."
I had it all planned out.

She reappeared, a little annoyed by my interruption.

"Why do you want to do that?"

"Oh, no reason ... I could use the cans though ..."

"You're up to something, mister, I hope it's something good."

"Don't worry, it is. You can have a ride on it when it's finished. It's a scooter from *Boys' Life.*"

"But you already have a scooter." Her voice was approaching exasperation.

"Not an orange-crate one that I made myself, with tin can headlights ..." My voice was almost succumbing to an unmanly whine.

"You really are up to something ... Just don't make a mess."

"I won't, promise." I ran into the kitchen to open two cans, pour the peas into the saucepan, cover it with a plate, put it into the fridge, wash the cans, strip off the paper covers, and run down the cellar steps out back.

As I got to the bottom of the stairs, I could hear the Forbeses' garage door closing, so I knew Bobby would be ready with the two-by-fours and the saw to cut them to the right size. I just hoped Mike could come up with his sister's skates. He did.

"It cost me, though, I have to be nice to her now for the rest of the summer," said Mike as he pried one of the skates into its two pieces with a skate key, handing the other to Bobby, who dropped three six-foot lengths of two-by-fours on the garage floor, along with some molding sticks. His father had everything.

"That'll be enough for six scooters," he said.

"What are the other sticks for?" asked Mike.

"Handlebars."

"I'm using paint stirrers on mine," I boasted, producing my treasures, along with the nails and hammer. I did not want to use the molding that served as my sword for such a non-martial purpose.

Robin and Greg showed up with their skates, and we got down to business. The first thing to do was saw the two-by-fours in half, which we did with a little trouble; not having a sawhorse, we had to use the garbage can, two sets of hands forming a loose vise. The cuts weren't perfect, but at least they were on the wood, not on anyone's hands. Like boys everywhere, we adhered to the implicit superstition that unless blood was drawn, no fun was had, but we were saving the mishaps for the ride down the big hill on the completed scooters.

Now that each of us had a base for our vehicle, we got to work installing the wheels. What a ruckus we made, five boys with hammers pounding on wood on a cement floor, some hits direct, some glancing off nails and thumbs. Grunts and satisfied sighs filled the suburban summer air.

I was never good at tools—a genetic lapse, I suppose, my father's side's tradeoff for glib tongue and smooth dance moves—and this morning's work went slowly for me. It took me a while to figure out that the skates could be held in place originally with the thin nails from the box marked BRADS and then secured more firmly with the longer nails. Getting the skates straight on the board was the trick, and my initial attempts using the big nails first ended in a design that would have made a scooter perfect for going in circles, but useless for going down hills or scooting in a straight line.

As we worked, Mike raised an interesting issue: "Hey, how do you steer one of these things? If the front wheel is nailed on straight, how do you steer?"

My red metal scooter had a completely turnable front wheel attached to a metal column connected to the handlebars, but I had learned that you could steer by shifting your weight. Not fast turns, but enough to keep from going into Springfield Road at the bottom of the hill. Beyond that street was an Esso station on a level space, after which the hill continued down Bishop Road. In the wintertime after a storm, when the snow was real slick and new, you could sled across the street, through the station and on down, as long as there were no cars, but in the summer there was often serious traffic, so being able to turn before you hit the street was a priority.

"Leaning," I responded, "you steer by leaning, lean to the right, go right, lean to the left ... "

"Let me guess," cracked Greg. "You go left."

"Right."

"No, left."

"OK, wise guy, correct, you go left."

Greg had finished his hammering, the wheels looked perfect—every nail driven straight. His indulgent parents had let him use really nice skates. I looked at my handiwork. I had used more nails than any of my friends, hammered at all angles, some straight in, some half in then bent over and hammered in sideways. I silently consoled myself that the extra nails would give it extra weight where it needed it most.

"Nice nail job," needled Greg. He was the youngest of us, which made his efficiency all the more grating. Since he was younger you couldn't really pick on him without looking like a bully, so he got away with boyhood murder.

"Hydronail transmission," I boasted. "What's it to ya?"

"Can I use some of the paint?" asked his older brother, also finished with the first step in the building process.

"Sure, I don't think we have any usable brushes, though."

"I'll get some." Off he went, just as Mike's sister Kathy and my sister Nancy came around the corner on their skates, keys hanging on cotton string around their necks.

"Hey, fellas, watcha doin', huh?" they called out in voices dripping with the treacle of human unkindness, knowing right well what we were doing but wanting to butt in as little sisters have done since time immemorial.

"Get lost, pipsqueak," said Mike.

"Mom," wailed Kathy in a fake hurt voice, "Michael's not keeping his skate promise."

"Michael," came a weary voice from the kitchen window.

"OK, OK, it's OK, Mom, I'm only kidding," he cried up, and then, in an ambiguous tone, "Come in, little sister, and see the General Scooters assembly plant. Here is where the wheels are attached to the chassis, and here"—pointing to the can of paint newly opened by Robin, who had returned from his house paintbrush in hand—"is our painting center."

"Very interesting," said Kathy in a grown-up voice, her hand stroking her chin like a supervisor from Detroit, "and where do you get your wheels?"

"Some are donated by kind family members, some are begged from family members, and some—"

"Are found under the cellar stairs," I added. "Tour's over, back to work everybody."

Robin was laying down newspaper on the garage floor to protect the oil stains from spilled paint. Greg was reading the *Boys' Life*, waiting for the rest of us to catch up, and Bobby was taking a bent nail out of his "chassis," wanting it to look perfect. I was back to my hydronail transmission.

"See you later, fellas," said Kathy in a slightly gloating tone, looking forward to a summer of enforced niceness from her brother. "We'll race you down the big hill when you're done." And off they went.

"Sisters," said Mike in exasperation, "You can't live with them, and you can't—"

"Have their old skates without 'em," I chimed in.

"Hey, you guys," said Greg, looking up from the magazine, "did you know that the fastest thing on land is a cheetah?"

"Great name for a scooter, I'll take it," I said, banging in another nail for ballast.

"Well, that's done," said Robin, showing off his handiwork, his paintbrush still dripping. "All I need now is an orange crate. When is the huckster coming?"

"Between three and four," said Mike, "usually."

"Think he'll have enough crates for us today?" asked Mike to no one in particular.

"Doubtful," said Greg. "Maybe we ought to go to Burrell's or Sloan's. I don't think the huckster is going to have five."

"Not empty, anyway," I added, bending my last nail and pounding it sideways into the wood. "I'll go with you. Anybody else?"

The rest were all still working on various aspects of their chassises, so Greg and I started up to the stores together.

The stores were located at the top of the hill, about three blocks up Springfield Road. This hill was a sort of continuation of the big and little ones that made our alleys so interesting, and it was the hill that gave our neighborhood one of its names— Clifton Heights. From the top of it you could see clear to the City Hall of Philadelphia, ten miles away.

There were two grocery stores in our neighborhood shopping district. Burrell's was just at the top of the hill. Greg slipped in the doors at the front of the store, and I continued down to Sloan's. It was the more interesting of the two markets.

The smell of the place was like no other in the world— well, at least the neighborhood. It was something like the smell of fresh produce and fresh meat, but it had another quality to it, perhaps emanating from the worn hardwood floors that Mrs. Sloan was sweeping as I came in. Mr. Sloan was waiting on a customer at the meat counter in the back, dressed in his customary straw skimmer, white shirt, black tie, and bloodied apron. They both spoke with accents.

"Good afternoon, Mrs. Sloan," I said in my best singsong voice, normally reserved for nuns entering the classroom at Holy Cross grade school. I noticed how out-of-season my manner was, but politeness was one of my best skills.

"Good afternoon, young man," she said, smiling, gold showing through her lips. "What can I do for you this fine afternoon? You got a note?" Sometimes I would come there with a note from my mother for what we needed, although more often we shopped at Burrell's, since it was closer to our house and, my mother always said, a little cheaper.

"No, ma'am, no note this time, I got a favor to ask you though," I said. "I need orange crates. Do you have any? Me and my friends are making orange-crate scooters."

"Meyer," she sang to her husband, "we got orange crates for the boy? They is building scooters."

"What we got is out back, if the trash man ain't come yet, should be something back there, some kind of crate. And welcome to them," he answered, throwing a piece of meat on the enameled metal scale. The woman he was waiting on looked at me, amused, smiling condescendingly.

"You can go through the back room there, young man, I hope you find something," said his wife, pointing me through, and returning to her task.

It was a thrill to go this way, past the giant refrigerator, through the storeroom full of shelves holding cans and cans and boxes of cans and other things, out to their little alley behind, just wide enough for the trash truck, which hadn't come yet.

There were several empty cardboard boxes, broken down and folded up, a few large aluminum trash cans filled with meat bones and scraps and packing material, and, thanks be to God, two wooden crates with pictures of sunny vineyards. Not orange crates, mind you, a little smaller, obviously holding grapes until recently, but good enough.

"Thank you," I shouted through the back door, and went down the alley with my booty.

Greg was waiting for me in front of Burrell's. He had three crates, two almost identical to mine, another one with a smiling orange-headed man wearing sunglasses and holding a flag with a bear on it—a real orange crate, bigger and stronger. It would go to him, the youngest of us.

"Five altogether, perfect, we won't need the huckster," I said, eyeing his bounty.

"I call the big one," he said, as we started down the street.

"Sure, sure, sure," was my jaded response.

When we got back to the garage, the other guys were lounging, their work finished.

"What took you guys so long?" chided Robin.

"We got ambuscaded by pirates," I responded, happy to use a word I had just encountered in my Uncle Bud's copy of *Tom Sawyer.*

"But we killed them all and made them give us their treasure. I call the big one," said Greg, the last phrase spoken quickly to preclude the others from "calling" it and making it theirs.

"You got it, little boy," smacked his older brother, choosing one of the grape crates. Bobby took the other one. I gave the less stained of mine to Mike, and we got to work.

I was smart enough to know that the handlebars should be put on first, and for this the smaller brads were sufficient. Although holding these in place was initially a problem, once the nail was started, they went in straighter than the sixteen-penny nails I had been using earlier in the day. (Luckily the sixteen-penny nails were longer than the pea cans were high, so I was temporarily spared further struggle with them.) I got a red reflector from my old J.C. Higgins and nailed it on the back of the two-by-four.

My hammering skills, if they had been tested by the attachment of skates to the bottom of the chassis, were further challenged by the placement of the "engine," as we came to call the crates, since the base, onto which we were nailing the engine, was a rolling one. It seemed every time I hit a nail, the two-by-four would move, and the nail would bend, but, using the skills of the morning, I kept on hitting, bending the nail further, and I entertained myself by making an interesting design with the bent nails, until I ran out. It wasn't as solid a connection as I would have liked, but I didn't want to spend any more time on it, because I would fall behind my friends on the production line.

Painting the engine was the final step, and this took longer than the other procedures, since we only had one paintbrush among us. By the time we were finished, dinner was ready, but before we all went in for the evening meal we had a chance to step back and look at our handiwork, each complimenting the others while at the same time knowing that his own was the best. Actually mine really *was* the best, since it had the "head-lights" and the reflector, although Greg's was the biggest, and Mike's the best painted. We wheeled them into our garage to dry, and we pledged to meet the next day at nine o'clock sharp to try them out together.

My sister Nancy ate the barest minimum of peas that night to test the sincerity of my promise to make my use of the two cans worthwhile, and she watched me with a strange smile as I placed them on my plate at a rate previously unknown at our table.

"So, what did you kids do today?" my father asked, as he did every night. I let my sisters speak first, since I wanted the last word, and politeness is the gambit of champions.

"I played with my dolls and colored and listened to the phonograph," offered my sister Mary, age five.

"Did you have a good time?"

"Yes, a pretty good time. I stayed in the lines and shared my toys with Cynthia"—the Bates brothers' sister.

"Mamamama" said my sister Karen, between spoonfuls of mushed carrots and peas from a jar. She was only five months old.

"Yes, I know you did," said my father lovingly to his baby daughter.

Nancy spoke up next. "I played jacks with Kathy Hall, and skated around the big block three times altogether."

"Did you fall?"

"Not once!" she answered proudly.

"Good girl. And what about you, Eddie?"

"Oh, nothing much," I said trying to sound nonchalant but in fact bursting with pride at the accomplishment drying in the garage, "Read *Boys' Life* and found a diagram that showed how to build a scooter out of orange crates and old skates and two-by-fours ..."

"And pea cans," continued my sister, passing me the bowl of cooling peas for my enjoyment. I shot her a brotherly look as I dutifully emptied the bowl.

"Where did you get the wood?" he asked.

"Mr. Forbes gave us the two-by-fours, and I got crates from Sloan's grocery, and nails from the dresser in the garage, and paint from there too. I hope you don't mind." It occurred to me that I really hadn't asked permission for the supplies.

"Not at all, not for a good project like a scooter, but don't you already have a scooter?"

"Yeah, but not one that I built myself."

"Of course. Did you find the hammer all right?"

"Yes, sir, but I think I may have used up all the nails."

"The sixteen-penny ones?"

"Yes, sir."

"That's what they're there for, to be used."

Whew, I thought to my scrupulous self.

"After dinner, maybe we can look at the work you did."

"No problem," I said, "No problem at all." I loved it when I did something that I could show off to my father. He was kind of a stern man, and his approval was very important to me.

After I had finished all the peas and helped clear the table, my father and I went down the cellar stairs and out to the garage. He slid the noisy door up, and I ducked in to turn on the light, grateful to my good memory that I didn't trip over any of the objects drying in the darkness.

"There it is," I announced, quickly pointing to mine before he could inappropriately and mistakenly admire the other kids' scooters.

"Very nice," he said, coming closer. "What interesting nail designs."

"Thanks."

"And yours even has headlights," he said, kind of proudly, I thought.

"Pea cans," I beamed. "Did you guess?"

"I was wondering why you ate so healthy tonight."

"I promised Mom."

"Now I get it."

"And look," I continued, "a reflector on the back."

"But you won't be driving this at night, will you?"

"Oh no," I promised. The thought hadn't occurred to me until then.

"Well, Eddie, this is very good work. When do you try it out?"

"We have a race tomorrow at nine sharp."

"Sorry I have to work."

"That's all right." Actually it was more than all right, his presence would have added too much pressure.

I turned off the light, and he closed the door behind us and locked it. "Want to keep the scooter safe." I felt a little honored by this gesture, the garage was rarely locked. We went back upstairs, where he bragged to my mother. Then he played with my sisters as I read *Boys' Life* until bedtime.

At nine o'clock the next morning I unlocked the garage and met my waiting friends in the alley. The paint was fairly dry, so we tried them out. I had learned the balance tricks with my red scooter, now abandoned in the basement, so I had a leg up on my friends, but pretty soon we were zooming up and down the flat alley behind our houses, the sweet noise of the skates amplified by the sounding boards of the wood. The handlebars on mine were lower than I would have liked, and I envied Greg's real orange crate—it placed his handles at a better position and he didn't have to lean over as much as I. But he didn't have headlights, so it evened out, I decided. The nails holding the engine to the chassis had not dug as deep as they should have, so there was more play than I would have liked in the connection, but I comforted myself with the illusion that I could steer the vehicle better than my friends. I quickly got the knack of steering by shifting my weight and could almost do it without holding on tightly.

After we had had some practice on the flat surface, Robin challenged us all to the inevitable race on the little hill. We took our positions, five across. Robin shouted up to Lee Comer, who lived at the top of the hill, to stick his head out the window and start the race. I looked down the hill, a little nervous, wondering how fast I would go and whether I would be able to stop at the street at the bottom. There was no brake on this thing, like there was on my red scooter.

"Ready!" came Lee's voice through the kitchen window screen, where he was imprisoned doing his summer school homework. "Set! Go!"

And we were off, five boys pumping downhill to gain speed. I was in the lead to begin with, Robin and Mike were almost even, then came Bobby Forbes. Surprisingly, Greg was last, his younger and therefore shorter legs unmatched to his scooter's size. Halfway down the hill there was a large crack in the cement. Trying to avoid it, Robin swerved into my scooter, then into the grass hill on the side of the alley where he wiped out, falling off his coaster and rolling in the grass, laughing, letting us know he wasn't hurt. Off-balance from the contact, mine began to wobble back and forth, and I tried to regain my balance, pulling hard on my handlebars and leaning this way and that to set it right. Greg had caught up to me, Mike passed us, and Bobby Forbes was now bringing up the rear.

As I attempted to fight the wobble, I felt a screeching vibration in the handlebars. It didn't take me long to discern the source—one of the nails holding the engine to the chassis. Things seemed to go into slow motion as first the one, then each of the sixteen-penny nails that looked so intricate in their overlapped design (which depended on a shallow dig into the two-by-fours) screeched out. With a final attempt at realignment, they let go entirely, and I had the odd sensation of taking off—only it was not me but my engine, which I now held in my hands, above my head, waving back and forth as I tried to maintain my balance down the hill, fighting the inclination to end the ride by leaning the contraption into the grass hill on my left.

Some natural instinct told me I would be better balanced with nothing in my hands, so I tossed the crate behind me and continued to careen down the hill, two feet still on the two-by-four; I was afraid to move either one, lest I lose my balance and fall entirely. I passed a surprised Greg and continued on, still afraid to try to stop, picking up speed since my wind resistance had become almost nil without the engine, and down toward Springfield Road, where I could see cars stopped at the red light, giving me just enough room to squeeze through to the other (thankfully empty) lane and into the Esso station. By shifting my weight I avoided hitting the amazed attendant and his pump. I rode beyond him to the sidewalk and, still descending the hill, began to approach the speed I had once attained while sledding the previous winter.

It was exhilarating. I could hear the cries of my friends behind me—"Go, Steamboat, go!"—as I swerved to avoid pedestrians. Not knowing how to stop, I let gravity do its work until the hill ended, and I slowed down enough to jump off. I picked up the skated two-by-four and started back up the hill, my knees shaking violently as the adrenalin pumped through my veins. I choked back an involuntary tear and tried to smile as my friends ran down to meet me.

"That was great," said Michael Hall, clapping me on the back.

"You did it this time, Steamboat," said Robin.

"I still won the race," said Greg defensively, "but you went one step beyond." Bobby was standing at the Esso station shaking his head, not quite believing what he had seen.

"Did you get hurt when you wiped out?" I asked Robin, trying to distract myself from the sense that I could burst out crying at any moment.

"Nope, got grass stains, though."

"Good, how's your scooter?"

"Better shape than yours," he joked.

"Yeah, though not as streamlined."

"How did you do it?" asked Bobby, finally.

"I didn't do it, really, Robin did it when he bumped into me."

"Sure, I'll take credit for what you did any day. You know what, you've invented a new kind of thing, a skating surfboard."

"Yeah, I guess I ought to patent it."

I would have made a lot of money if I had. Within two years, they were all the rage—but without the reflector.

Mass at the Convent

I only saw the back of the convent once, and never all the way around the back, just a quick peek as I was walking quickly by on the way to Frankie Clearfield's house for a Boy Scout patrol meeting one time in sixth grade. Taking a shortcut through the church property, I happened to glance at a clothes-line that was fairly obscured by the trees, and saw some white garments hanging on a line, but I didn't gaze long enough to figure out what the garments were, or what part of the sisters they might have supported or covered, but just kept right on going, because what I was doing was almost a sin, I was sure, seeing nuns' underwear. It hadn't even occurred to me that the Mercy nuns wore underwear. No way they went to the bathroom, after all. They were too perfect to have to do such a mundane and disgusting thing; besides, how could they with all the clothes they had on?

The convent was a scary place, not because the nuns were evil, but because there were very few reasons one had to go there—and all of them had emotional ramifications. The least scary reason was Hallowe'en, ironically, because it was then that the nuns seemed to have the least power over us. Showing up at their residence in a costume was not really a homework assignment, and their gaze at our work on that night was most benign, offering the immediate gratification of a lollipop, whether our work was really good or not. Even though they gave out lousy candy—lollipops!—a visit to the convent on Hallowe'en was the high point of traipsing through the neighborhood, though in my later years when quantity of sweets became more important than quality of time, I skipped the convent, leaving it to my younger siblings and neighbors.

If the nuns were somewhere between one's own mother and the Blessed Mother in Heaven, Hallowe'en was the most signal time. On this one night, they were as approachable as any neighborhood mother being hit up for a peanut butter and jelly sandwich; this made them kind of vulnerable in a way. Besides, they couldn't punish us if our costumes weren't that good—and they raved about each costume anyway.

There was always a quorum of them on duty for this yearly event, so the job of guessing our names was manageable. We would stand in line for a moment just inside the door and approach the ad hoc panel, who would make an appropriate fuss, and then give us our reward, sometimes stopping to have a picture taken by a proud or pushy parent, and then on to the next one, while some of us dawdled and drank cider. They were always in a jovial mood: even the short eighth-grade nun lost her defensive scowl that normally kept the big boys in line, there weren't that many eighth-graders around to be spoiled by her good humor that night anyway.

One way you knew you were in the convent was from the squeaking sound coming from your shoes as you walked. If kidnappers blindfolded me and brought me into that foyer, and down the hall, I would know exactly where I was from the squeak of my shoes. The hallway floors of the convent were like glass. Not slippery, necessarily, but almost completely reflective. The tiles were asphalt, just like the kind in our kitchen. It was my job to clean and wax the ones in our house, but my results were never like the floors of the convent. How they got that way, I'm not sure, but I imagine it was the sisters, down on their hands and knees, buffing the floor by hand. For hours.

The impeccability of the floors, of course, was in keeping with the rest of the image I had of the nuns, perfect creatures with never a hem falling nor a speck of dust on a black sleeve. Later on, when I was teaching in a Catholic high school, my jacket would be covered with chalk at the end of the day, but I rarely saw it on the black habits of the Mercy nuns. Their starched linen bibs, wimples and headdresses were never soiled. I still don't know how they did it.

There were other times in the year, besides Hallowe'en, when a visit to the convent was necessary, which usually indicated a behavior problem. Being called there for a conference meant that you were in extra big trouble. Right inside the foyer there were two stairways, one leading down to the Hallowe'en room, and the other leading up to a hallway that held four doors, behind each of which was a small parlor, with a glass-perfect floor, a little rug, and several sofas and chairs. These rooms were well kept, their primary purpose not discipline but visits with members of the nuns' families. For a young woman in those days, joining the convent meant that you couldn't go home again, literally, except at the death of a parent, so any contact with the family took place in these little rooms, and that very seldom. For a person outside the family, however, sitting in these rooms was quite foreboding.

I only got in such trouble once in my grade-school career, and it happened late in my time there, eighth grade to be exact, by which time a visit to the convent was not so daunting, since my class, Baby Boom pioneers that we were, pushing the envelope of space, had our classroom in the basement. There was no room for us in the school building.

But there was another visit to the convent, one that I will never forget, and it was not for discipline that I was there, unless the service of God's altar is discipline itself.

I had been chosen to be an altar boy in fifth grade. It was a great honor that I reckoned was simply a result of my being among the smartest kids in my class. As it turned out, geography had a hand in it too: I lived close to the church property and could get there easily no matter what the weather. I knew there was a nuns' Mass every day in the convent chapel, but this was normally assisted by one of the Colonial Park kids, who only had to cross a yard or two to get there.

But one morning in sixth grade, it fell to me to cover for Mike Menseck, the assigned altar boy who was sick, and I got up very early to perform my task. It was still dark as I approached the door of the convent that winter morning and rang the bell.

"Trick or treat," I said under my steaming breath as I waited. I heard the squeaks of the shoes on the floor before I saw the shadow of the nun in the newly turned-on lights. A curtain was drawn back, just enough for a peek at the bell-ringer, and then the door opened. The scent of wax and Ivory soap embraced me and drew me in the door.

"Good morning." The voice sounded much more awake than mine.

"Good morning, Sister, I'm here to serve Mass, I'm Edward Stivender."

"Of course, Edward, your sister Nancy is in my class, I'm Sister Mary Joan, follow me." She squeaked down the corridor ahead of me. I walked on tiptoe so that my shoes wouldn't make a sound and disturb the silence of the place any further. I was a stranger here, I knew, a kind of foreigner that didn't—wouldn't ever—belong, and whose presence was an indulgence wrought by the presumed need of this female community for a male link to the worldwide universal church which had at its center the simple feast of bread and wine, which could only be hosted by a man, albeit a man in a dress. And that man fit the role of surrogate father, brother, perhaps son, on some sublime level Best Man of their spiritual husband Christ, or maybe Christ Himself, chaste spouse to so many women and I the servant of the man and of the house at once. The air of a place with many religious women and one priest is a strange and vital air, one which I didn't understand then but felt strongly. None of these women needed a man of their own to complete their life as married women might, but the presence of a man in short hushed moments somehow filled a gap. Scientists today could point to pheromones and chemicals in the air to explain this phenomenon, but no scientist could deny the existence of such a thing.

At the end of the corridor I could see a door inlaid with stained glass, beyond which I knew was the chapel. Sister stopped just short of that door and showed me to a small sacristy where the priest's vestments were laid out on a table, next to which there was a rack of servers' cassocks and surplices, almost unrecognizable as such, because of the care with which these garments were hung, not thrown willy-nilly on the rack by careless boys, as was the case in the church sacristy. In addition, these surplices were starched and ironed crisp. The garments fairly crackled as I dressed.

Father MacKenzie came in and started vesting as I stood by. Outside I could hear the nuns arriving, a thousand subtle squeaks, like crickets' horns announcing the arrival of the ladies of the court of the most high King. I helped Father with his cincture, and we were ready. We entered through the stained glass door and approached the altar.

The room was smaller than any I had gone to Mass in, and the nuns' presence right behind me added to the normal pressure that serving Mass brought with it. I was on my best behavior, saying my responses clearly and loud enough for all to hear, though I knew I was really superfluous in this role, for behind me was the nun who had taught me the Latin, Sister Regina Christi, as well as the rest of them with sweet dog-eared missals doing the responses along with me, silently or almost silently, their lips barely moving. Some of the older ones knew the Mass by heart after all, but I was pleased to be there, knowing that a mistake on my part would not affect the grace of the Mass one bit, borne as it was upon black wings of extreme faith far beyond my own.

As Father read the epistle, I waited behind him, taking in the beauty of the room. The altar was lovely—laid out with crisper linens than I had ever seen—but it was a stained glass piece above the altar that caught and held my attention for the rest of the Mass.

For there was a rendering of a great bird brooding over a nest of her young with wings outstretched—ah! bright wings—and the chicks seemed to be suckling. My first response was the scientific critical response, that only mammals feed their young in such a way, and birds don't have breasts, not even pelicans, as I now recognized this one to be. But then I looked closer and saw the technique that allowed the suckling to occur—the pelican had drops of blood dripping from its breast; it was piercing its own breast with its beak to let the blood flow to nourish its children.

With this insight, a mixture of horror and fascination welled up inside me. What love of a creature for its children! But what a price to pay! Why was this picture in the chapel? It wasn't a saint, or from the Bible—at least I hadn't encountered any scripture like it.

As Father gave a short sermon to the sisters, I continued to grapple with the question. Was it a pagan architect's plot to bring in such a strange non-Christian symbol? I looked at the nuns, listening to Father, their eyes cast down at their white starched bibs.

And then it hit me—a strange thought, even more troubling than paganism. The nuns were the pelicans and we students were their young. They were giving their lifeblood for our education. And the pelican was the symbol of that sacrifice.

Some rational part of me knew this was too strange, but still another part of me wished I had looked closer at the garments on the clothesline. Feeling confused by my inner voices, I started saying Hail Marys, my favorite remedy, and glanced up at the crucifix just below the stained glass window to quiet my thoughts. The figure of Jesus had blood dripping from His head as well as from the lance wound in His side. My whirling brain finally calmed down when it caught the connection. The pelican was Christ, of course; her body and blood the sacrament of the bread and wine; her children, us Catholics.

His sermon finished, Father approached the altar, and I got the cruets from the credence table, ready to assist him. After he had mixed the water and wine and made his lavabo, I returned to my place behind him to ring the bell for the consecration. And when he raised the bread above his head, I saw the three levels of the intended symbol—Pelican, Savior, and unleavened bread—and was thankful for the simple elegance of this last. And as I held the communion plate at each nun's starched-linened neck, I was grateful to be a small part of this simple mystery of gender, love, and sacrifice.

At the Academy of Music

*M*y father loved classical music. I don't know where he acquired the taste for it. Having been raised in an orphanage in South Carolina, he might have had access to it there, but I doubt it. He joined the Navy at a very young age, a way of escaping the orphanage, no doubt, but I don't know what kind of classical music they played in the boiler room of the USS *Phoenix* as he checked the gauges. I don't think he got it from my mother, whose tastes tended toward the Big Band sound. Perhaps it was genetic.

One Saturday afternoon in December of my twelfth year, Santa brought an early Christmas present. At least my father said it was from Santa, though it still had store tags on it. Dad set the thing—a real piece of furniture it was, all wrapped in plastic and smelling like a furniture store—against the front wall in the living room, right under the window. I had run in from outside when I saw the commotion of the delivery. My sisters were there too, hugging my mother's legs, afraid of the new thing, perhaps because it was so obviously important to my father.

"Well, here it is, kids, an early present from Santa," he said, puffing from the climb up the front steps and wiping his brow with a clean white handkerchief. (He always carried two, one for himself and one in case some girl needed one. He urged me to do the same. I still try to.)

"What is it, a television?" asked my sister Mary.

"No, it's not a television, although its about the same size..."

"No screen, though, right?" I pointed out wisely.

"That's right, Eddie, also bigger speakers than the television," he stated as he began to unwrap the plastic that was taped around it. "It's a Hi-Fi—short for High Fidelity phonograph. It has two kinds of speakers, big ones called woofers and little ones called tweeters."

I laughed out loud. "Tweeters—what a funny name."

"And woofers isn't?" chided my sister Nancy, just one year younger.

"Woof," said Mary, imitating a dog.

"Tweet," I responded.

"Goo goo gah," said my infant sister Karen from my mother's arms.

"You're kidding, but you're not far off the track, you kids. The woofers are speakers that are good for a deep dog's voice, and bass and baritone singers, and the tweeters are good for bird whistles and the voice of a soprano. Put them all together and you get a full rich range of sound from highs to lows," he said, sounding like a sales manual. He had all the plastic off and was working on taking the wrapping off the needle arm and spindle. I edged a little closer to see the insides. It had more dials than our other record players, and the arm was slimmer.

"The main thing to remember, kids, is, *this is not a toy.*" This we could tell from the care he was taking, but he always liked things clear. "It's only for Mommy and Daddy to play until you get a little older." (Or until *it* gets a little older, I thought to myself, knowing a little about how things worked in the world.)

The plastic and inner wrapping gone, he began to unwind the electrical power cord, moving toward the wall socket as he unravelled it. He plugged it in. Then he reached into a thin paper bag and produced a large flat object that I knew immediately was a record, an LP. On the cover was a picture of a balding white-haired man in black tails strenuously waving his arms around, obviously a conductor. My father carefully drew out the record, housed in a paper sleeve, which he removed as he continued.

"You must never touch the playing surface of the record, only the label, the red paper near the center hole, and the edge." As he spoke he demonstrated. We held our breath, hoping he wouldn't drop it. His hands were shaking, either from excitement or exhaustion from carrying the thing up the steps. Taking the record now with both hands on the edges, he carefully placed it on a complex-looking rod above the turntable, where it hooked a quarter of the way down the rod, and stayed there. Then he maneuvered another metal piece so that it held the disc horizontal, a few inches above the turntable. Fearing that the mechanism was defective since the record wasn't dropping down, I asked, "Is it broken?"

My father laughed. "No, son, this is one of the great things about it. It has a record-changing mechanism that holds several records up and drops them down one at a time. Watch."

He put his hand on a dial in the well, and turned. Mary immediately said, "Red light." I looked down to see that she was pointing to something on the front of the machine. Sure enough, there was a little red light in the lower right hand corner of the fabric covering the speakers. It was glowing, as it had not been doing before.

"Right, Mary, it tells us when the machine is on," he said supportively.

I was focused back on the workings of the spindle and needle arm. I could hear the motor hum, the shift of gears and cogs; the needle arm lifted and paused in midair. Suddenly the record dropped. I jumped. Then the needle arm moved, lowering itself right on the edge of the record. There was a hiss, and then the Philadelphia Orchestra was in the room with us—at least that's how it seemed. My father adjusted the dials meticulously, his ear cocked to hear the nuances that were beyond my understanding. My two sisters started doing ballet dance moves around the living room floor. I sat down in front of the speakers to get the full effect.

"Not too close, Eddie," warned my mother, rhythmically rocking my baby sister. I moved away a half-inch to make her happy. Then I closed my eyes and soared on the sounds coming from Santa's early present. I was an eagle above a multicolored valley of changing hues. I had become a pretty accomplished daydreamer by that time, so I had some practice, but this was different, I was soaring on the winds of music. If you wanted to place your mind in a certain way, you could almost see the musicians. I opened my eyes and reached for the album cover and indeed saw on the back the musicians sitting in black suits, holding their instruments—so many different kinds. I imagined I could hear each one clearly.

I looked back to see what my parents were doing. They were just standing there, my father behind my mother, hands around her waist, as she held Karen. My sisters danced around the three of them, and they were smiling. I closed my eyes again and went back to my private soaring.

Soon I felt my sisters sitting on either side of me, panting from their dance. To keep them entertained, I pretended my hands were ballet dancers, two extended fingers the legs, doing a high-kick cancan. They joined me in this improvisational dance and soon there was a pas de six on the floor in front of us, moving back and forth in time to the music, coming together for a final crescendo, and falling together in a clump as the music ended. We were surprised by the applause above our heads. Our two-person audience was beaming with some kind of pride, either at the fact that they had children, or that the children were so musically talented, or that they were getting along at all.

"Santa Claus sure knows how to pick a present," I volunteered.

"Even if it's not a toy," said my sister, Nancy, wisely.

"Woof, woof, tweet, tweet," said Mary.

I'm hungry, wailed Karen, in her own musical language, decoded swiftly by our attentive mother.

One day as I was listening to the Hi-Fi, my dad asked me if I wanted to go to see the orchestra in person.

"Would I? I sure would, Dad, but it probably costs too much."

"Not necessarily, son. I know a way to get in for a dollar apiece, but we'll have to stand in line."

"I've been doing that since first grade." My Catholic education had served me well. I had been standing in line since the first day of school. Doing so with my father would be better than any line at school, however. Doing anything with my father was a great pleasure. I was a little afraid of him, and interested in getting his approval. I knew that he loved me, but he was a strict man; he preferred that I address him, and all male adults, with "Sir," for instance. Being alone with him, however, would be an honor and, I hoped, great fun.

I think on some level we were afraid of each other—I of his sternness, he of my Catholicism. Sometimes I wondered if he regretted turning us over to the Church. It was a whole aspect of his family's life that he did not share. Whereas some fathers, nominally Catholic, would sit in their cars as their families attended Mass inside, he stayed home while the rest of us walked. There was never any resistance to our churchgoing, but I was never clear about how he felt.

My parents had a mixed marriage.

"Good, because we'll have to stand in line for about an hour."

"That's no problem, the May Procession is longer than that."

"But it's also a little bit warmer in May. This is November, after all, and it could be chilly."

"My winter coat from last Christmas still fits me fine. I'll wear warm socks," I added anxiously, afraid of losing the offer.

"All right, then, we'll leave right after dinner on Saturday afternoon."

Just then my sisters came in from outside.

"Hey Nancy, I'm going to the orchestra on Saturday with Dad," I burst out gleefully, then realizing there was an implicit slight to her in my announcement, I added, as sincerely as I could, "Wanna come?"

"To the orchestra? On Saturday?" She was thinking. "Nah, I don't think so, me and Kathy Hall are going to Cynthia's pajama party."

Whew, I was saved. On the one hand, I really liked my sister, but on the other hand, spending time alone with my dad was important to me.

"Hey, Mom," I yelled, running into the kitchen, "I'm going to the orchestra with Dad on Saturday."

"Very good, Eddie, but you won't miss Confession, will you?"

I wouldn't dream of missing Confession if I could help it, unless there was a really good reason. Seeing the orchestra was not a really good reason, apparently. It didn't occur to me that my mother wanted me to be in a state of grace in case I was killed in the city, which she considered a more dangerous place than my father did. We both knew that if I died in the evening after Confession, I would go directly to Heaven.

"Oh no, I'll still go to Confession."

"Good boy, and we'll have dinner right after so you guys can get downtown in plenty of time," she said benevolently.

I ran back to the living room where my father was dealing Old Maid cards to my sisters and told him the news about early dinner.

"Great, son, now I think we should get dressed up for the orchestra, coat and tie and all, we don't want to look like farmers, so make sure your school clothes are cleaned and your shoes are shined. Is your overcoat in good shape?"

"I'm sure it is, haven't really worn it since it got cleaned at the beginning of the school year," I said, going to the closet near the steps to reveal a coat still in the plastic bag from the one-hour martinizing place.

I was thankful that I went to Catholic school, then, because the dress code included a coat and tie, every day. If my public friend Rob Keating's dad wanted to take him to the orchestra, he'd have to buy a coat and tie, or else look like a farmer, but I was all set. Shining my shoes is something I did anyway, and was pretty good at, actually, since I had a job at the barber shop doing it, and my father had set me up with a professional shoeshine kit for that purpose.

I ran upstairs to start shining my good shoes. I had three pairs of shoes at the time, as well as a pair of sneakers. I opened the closet door in my bedroom and surveyed the possibilities. Two brown, one black pair. I took the black pair, which I wore with my scout uniform and on Sundays and for the May Procession, and I began to polish. When I was finished, I ran back downstairs and announced to everyone that I was ready. My sisters didn't care, but my father looked up from the game and said, "I'm proud of you."

The rest of the week went quickly. I bragged about it to my friends, though the only one who was in any way duly impressed was Joe Tranchitella, who always listened to musical comedy shows and went downtown occasionally to see one. He told me not to miss seeing Billy Penn at night. Billy Penn was the statue on top of the Philadelphia City Hall. I wasn't sure where it was in relation to the Academy of Music. He told me to go out on Broad Street and look up.

The morning of the concert I awoke early. You might have thought it was Christmas, excited as I was. My father was already at work, at his third job—the Mid-City Health Club, which he and a partner had opened at 1718 Sansom Street downtown. During the week he worked nine to five at Publicker's Distillery, and at night at E.J. Korvette's, a department store. He provided for his family well.

My mother was sweeping the living room with the noisy Hoover by the time I had brushed my teeth and showered and come downstairs. I offered to help. I must admit it was the first time I had done so, but I was feeling in a benevolent mood. She was surprised at my offer, but took me up on it and went on to the task of cleaning the venetian blinds while I struggled with the vacuum. I had to turn it off several times to keep the corners of the rug from being sucked in. Each time I turned it off I could hear the Hi-Fi, which was playing along unheard over the sound of the vacuum.

When I was finished, I wound the cord about the handle of the machine and listened as a black voice crooned about coffee and the Java Jive, and on to "Little Coquette." Every time I heard this word, I thought of the frozen chicken croquettes that we sometimes had for dinner, and couldn't understand why a guy would call his girlfriend that. At the end of the song the guy sings, "You'll know, little coquette, I love you," and I always felt that it was a kind of radio ad for frozen dinners, or could have been. The singer was part of a group called The Ink Spots, and their album was a favorite of my parents, who had expanded the repertoire of the record collection beyond the classical, and our living room was turned into a dance hall several times a week, as they waltzed all over the living room floor. When Dad was working, the records helped my mother get into a cleaning mood.

I rolled the cleaner back to its place at the top of the cellar stairs and noticed the ironing board was up. Hanging from the end of it was a newly starched and ironed shirt of mine.

"Is this for tonight?" I called into the other room.

"Yes, it is. Are your shoes shined?" came the response.

"Yes, ma'am, spit-shined, I can see my reflection in them," I answered proudly. "Anything else I can help you with?"

"I don't think so, Eddie, why don't you go out and play?" I think she wanted me out of her hair, so she could get some real work done. The Al Hibbler album had just dropped down, and he was singing, "Don't get around much any more" in a voice deeper than anyone in my neighborhood.

I quickly ate some cereal and then ran down the cellar steps and into the backyard. The day was crisp, but nobody was out yet. I walked up and down the alley.

"Ee-yah-kee!" I yelled, singing out our block call, stolen from "Lassie."

"Ee-yah-kee!" came a reply.

I looked toward the source—the Bateses' kitchen window. Robin and Greg were eating breakfast.

"Can you come out and play today?" I shouted up. It was a ritual, this friend-calling, fairly programmed, the last line even had a kind of tune to it.

"Be out in a minute," called Greg, gulping down some toast.

Michael Kanouse came out of his house with a football.

"Heads up!" he called as he threw. I caught the ball and threw it back. He had to run for it, but he got it. Now the distance between us made the throws interesting. Robin and Greg came out, Michael Hall appeared, then Bobby Forbes. We had enough for a game, three on each side.

The row homes that our families lived in each sported a small back yard three times as long as it was wide, big enough for a good game of catch. But together, side by side, there was a whole field for touch football, with one goal line at Masons' boundary (the end house) and the other at the line between the Forbes and Bates properties, with the Bates yard as the end zone. Jimmy Smith's parents (on the far side of the Bates property) had set up a big hedge, selfishly fencing their own land, so we couldn't use Michael Kanouse's yard on the other side of that, but it worked out. A touchdown would take just two short passes or one long pass, but running was always possible.

We chose out sides—Robin, Bobby Forbes and me against Greg and the two Mikes. Greg was the most dangerous player—he was skinny and fast. We kicked off and Greg caught it, running nearly halfway till I tagged him.

"Nunh-unh," he protested, "that was only one hand."

"Quit complaining," I shot back. "I got you with two hands fair and square."

They huddled. We huddled, sort of. The defending team really didn't have a huddle. Robin, our captain—that is, the guy who had done the choosing out, the bigger of us—pointed at me and said, "Steamboat, you cover Greg. Bob, you cover Mike Hall—I'll go in."

These assignments were foregone conclusions. I always would get Greg, since I was second fastest on the block, although Mike Hall, as third fastest, would give Forbesy a run for his money.

"Set one, set two, hike," said Kanouse. The two other teammates made for the Masons' property, covered well by me and Bob. Michael Kanouse was almost blocked by Robin. He overthrew, and Greg missed it by a mile.

"Nice try, Greg," I said, sportsmanlike, glad that my words had an edge since a *really* nice try would have made the catch.

They huddled. We waited.

Same play. Same results.

"Nice try."

"Shut up."

This was their last real chance, they'd have to kick it if they didn't make this one. As we waited for their huddle, I looked up and surveyed the sky. A perfect fall day, a few fast clouds, a few maple leaves making their final pirouettes. I thought of my symphonic flight with the Hi-Fi earlier in the week, but realized that the music these leaves were dancing to was much more rhythmic and faster than mine. I tried to imagine the music that drove the leaves ...

"Hike!" I woke up as a flash of yellow that was Greg's hair zoomed past me. I turned to chase him, but he was already in the end zone, his hand waving to signal the quarterback that he was open. I ran a few steps, then turned around to block the pass, but it was above my head and into Greg's hands before I even realized what was happening.

Greg was running back to his teammates, elated. "Nice try," he said as he passed me.

"I didn't even try," I called after him. "I let you get that one. It was a mercy catch."

"Sure," was the collective response from their team.

Robin and Bob were glaring at me.

"Falling asleep on us, Steamboat."

"Yeah, sorry."

There was no kick for an extra point—we had no goal posts to kick through, so we walked back and lined up to receive. Forbesy received and Robin and I blocked as well as we could, but sneaky Gregory Bates got around us. We huddled. The options discussed in the huddle of a team of three on a field less than twenty yards long were limited.

"All right," said Robin, "go out for a pass, but cross and pick each other's cover off." He drew it on his sweatshirt, his back to the other team, who were straining to hear the plan, stepping over the line of scrimmage to do so.

We lined up, Robin gave the signals, Bobby hiked it, and off we went. We ran down the sidelines and into the middle, where we collided and fell to the ground as the ball was thrown to where I would have been if I wasn't on my back looking up at the symphony of wind, leaf, and cloud, laughing and trying to stop.

"Are you all right, Bob?" I asked, getting up.

"Yeah, you?" He wasn't laughing but was obviously not hurt, more chagrined than I.

"Nice pick-off," said Greg.

"It's our plan to make you overconfident, and then squash you like a bug when you least expect it," I said, trying to sound menacing and hide the tears behind my laughter. I would never become a good athlete because of this relative sense of things I had: a comic moment like that was as valid to me as a successful play.

The rest of the game didn't get any better, and they won by three touchdowns. Afterwards, we rode our bikes down to Darby Creek and skipped stones and talked. I bragged about what I would do that night.

"Do you like that kind of music?" asked Mike Hall.

"Yeah, I like all kinds of music, including classical, but the best part of it all is going downtown with my dad. Have you ever been downtown?" I asked, trying to impress my friends as to how lucky I was.

"Been to the Mummers' Parade," said Greg.

"Been to the Navy Yard with my father," bragged Michael Kanouse.

"We've all been there," said Bobby Forbes.

"Not us," said Greg. Mr. Bates was the only one of the fathers on the block that wasn't in the Navy, an interesting demographic fact. The rest of our dads had served together in some capacity or other. Mr. Forbes and my dad served in the Mediterranean during Korea. Mr. Bates had been in the Army, I think.

"Besides," covered Greg, "the Navy Yard isn't really downtown, it's in South Philly."

As we talked and boasted and covered, I looked into the Creek and saw another dance going on. A slower one than the one in the sky above my head during football, more of an adagio than an allegro. (I had been reading the album covers of the classical records and had found out the difference.) Maple leaves in various degrees of red and yellow were making their way over the mossy rocks of the creek, bending and swaying like dancers and then joining their mates to make an undulating collage as they were trapped by a row of rocks just downstream. Mike was trying to land a skipped stone on the mess of leaves, with little luck. They kept going beyond and plunking into the turbulence on the other side of the rocks.

"There, I did it," he shouted and pointed to the flat stone just beginning to sink among the leaves.

"Nice shot," I said. It was. We all started aiming for it, with little success. I was beginning to get nervous about the time. None of us had a watch, but I knew it must be after two o'clock.

"Hey youse guys, I gotta go get cleaned up and all, see you later."

"All right, have fun tonight downtown."

"Don't do anything I wouldn't do," said Robin.

"And if you do, name it after me," said his younger brother.

I was pretty sure he didn't know what it meant, I had only found out a few weeks before when Danny Kelly had explained it to me. I got on my bike, a 26" J.C. Higgins red balloon-tire model and started up the hills toward home. When I got there it was three o'clock. I was right on schedule.

"Hi, Mom, I'm home," I called to her in the kitchen as I went up the two flights of steps to my room to change. From the banging noises coming from the kitchen I figured out she was making a piecrust, which she always made from scratch. Her timing was not much of a surprise since the Sunday before we had made our annual trip out to Linvilla Orchards in the countryside beyond Media to pick up her favorite kind of apples—Jonathan, I think they were. Later on, in the '60s, when there was the old saw about American values being tied up with Ma and Apple Pie, I think I missed the edge of the critique, because I could think of no better combination for a fall afternoon.

Upstairs I showered and got dressed for Confession, saving my really good clothes, including the starched and ironed shirt that now hung on a hanger on the doorknob of my bedroom, for later. The priest couldn't really see what you were wearing, and the church rules for dress on Saturday afternoon were less stringent than those for Sunday morning.

I was the first person in the church that afternoon, and had time for an examination of conscience. Didn't even have a good sin of disobedience this week. Didn't fight with my sister, didn't take God's name in vain, went to church on Sunday, didn't kill anybody, didn't commit adultery—how could I? I wasn't an adult—didn't steal or lie or cheat ...

Wait a minute, how about the football game? On that first play, did I really get Greg with both hands? I certainly got him full on the back with my right hand, but my left hand had really just caught clothing, no skin or bone, and he really wasn't down. Thank Heaven, a sin, I wouldn't have to make any up this time.

Did I covet my neighbor's goods? Nah, my neighbors didn't really have anything I needed. I had the good dad, the mom who made the best apple pie, the three fairly decent sisters—I was pretty lucky. A little voice warned me against the incipient sin of Pride that might come from all this good fortune, but I waved it off. I considered coveting one neighbor's wife, the prettiest mother on the block, but I was too young to have the wherewithal to really covet anybody, so that was no good. Nope, just the one possible infraction of the seventh commandment: I had sort of cheated in a football game.

The priest was bored, as usual, with my sin, and I was out of there after only three Hail Marys and home well before four o'clock. The apple pie was under way in the oven, and my father was home. Everything was on schedule; we had to be in line by six-thirty if we wanted a good seat.

The normal meal on Saturday was steak, bought at the Acme on sale, baked potatoes, and a delicious string bean dish my mother made from french-fried onion rings and cream of mushroom soup. I always thought it was her own invention until recently, when I saw the dish advertised in a Durkee Foods commercial on TV. Perhaps they got the recipe from her.

The meal was very good. The pie, on the other hand, was outrageous, still hot, with a dip of Breyer's vanilla ice cream, the kind with the little black beans showing. All this, and a concert with my dad ahead—I truly was blessed (and in a state of grace, as well).

I made a vain gesture to help clean up after but was shooed by my mother, so I ran upstairs to get dressed and ready.

In the bathroom, I brushed my teeth, then oiled my hair with Wildroot Cream Oil and tried to get my cowlicks under control.

"Dad," I called out, "can I use some Old Spice?"

"Did you shave?" His voice had a surprised chuckle.

"Well, not exactly," I answered, surveying my smooth preadolescent face, looking vainly for something to shave. There was gossamer there that some day would be whiskers, but not today.

"Go ahead, son, but save some for me."

"Yes, sir." I shot a drop or two out of the white bottle into my hand and then slapped my face several times. Now I smelled like my father and Father Gatens, the altar boy priest at church. I placed the little plastic cork back in the bottle and returned it to the medicine closet. The thought of pouring some down the drain so he would need a new bottle by Christmastime entered my brain, but I knew that wasting it would be a venial sin, so I refrained.

Dressed and scented, I went downstairs and watched TV with my sisters until my father came down. We put on our overcoats—mine smelled like the cleaners—and down the front stoop steps to the Plymouth Cedarwood sitting on Springfield Road. Then we were off.

On the way downtown, a ride of about a half an hour, we played our favorite radio game, punching the buttons to change the channel in mid-sentence, mid-song, or even mid-word. Since the six o'clock news was on most of the stations we had a great time scrambling the newscasts.

"There was a three-car accident at the corner of Market and Fifty-third Street today, no one was seriously—over under around and through Pall Mall's fine—policemen reported a holdup of the Pennsylvania National—clouds for most of the day tomorrow, but for tonight—three o'clock rock, four o'clock five o'clock six o'clock—out of control when he fell asleep at the—game was tied fourteen-fourteen." We laughed the whole half-hour, and then we were downtown.

"Here's the Schuylkill River," he said as we went over a bridge, the lights of center city shining before us. "It separates center city from West Philadelphia."

My father knew the town very well and knew where to park on a side street for free. We got out of the car and began to walk. Lots of people were out, wrapped in coats and scarves—there was a serious wind blowing—but none of this bothered me, I was with my dad. We came to a major street with five lanes of traffic and brighter street lamps than the one we had been on. At the corner, as we waited for the light, I looked up the street to my right and saw a tall spire-like building that seemed to be standing in the middle of the street about four blocks away. On top of it stood a man dressed in old-time clothing carrying a scroll in one hand, his other hand extended as though to calm the taxis that were honking below.

"Is that Billy Penn, Dad?"

"That's Billy Penn all right, standing on top of City Hall."

"Why is it in the middle of the street?"

My father laughed. "Well, he's so big and important that the street goes around him. That's kind of the center of center city."

My father was a good teacher, he always treated my questions with respect, and took care to answer them when he could. And he could answer any question about this adopted city of his, he was a man about town. Which made me a kid about town.

"See the big brick building over there, with all the gas lanterns, just this side of the fancy hotel? That's the Academy of Music."

There were a few people milling about in front. We were early, but by the time we got around to Locust Street, there was already a line of people standing near a door that said AMPHI-THEATRE. We got in line behind an older couple who were engaged in lively conversation in a foreign language. When they felt our presence, they paused and both looked behind and bowed slightly. The man said in a rich accent, "Welcome to the line."

I nodded a shy thank-you, and my father said, "It's pretty early for it to be this long."

"Yah, this Entremont brings them out, he's a real favorite now." We both nodded and they went back to their conversation. My father explained the reference to the name by pointing to a poster in a lit glass case.

"Phillippe Entremont is the piano soloist, son, see his name right under Ormandy's. He's very popular, this concert was sold out weeks ago."

I looked at the bill, trying to read the other names. "What instrument does Rachmaninoff play?"

"Rachmaninoff is the composer, though he probably did play piano sometimes. He wrote one of the pieces. He won't be here tonight." He paused. "Except in spirit. I mean his work will be here, but not him," said my father, trying to be precise.

The couple in front of us were arguing about something, and the name Stokowski kept coming up.

"Who is Stokowski?" I whispered.

"Leopold Stokowski," my father whispered back. "He used to have Ormandy's job. He was in that Disney cartoon *Fantasia*, the guy with long white hair that shakes Mickey Mouse's hand."

"Oh, yeah," I said, pretending to remember.

There stepped up behind us another couple, not as old as the ones in front, dressed warmly in suburban car coats. They looked ready for a football game.

"Welcome to the line," I said to them when they nodded hello, tempted to imitate the accent of our other neighbors.

"Well, thank you," said the woman. "What a gentleman you are."

I could feel my face getting red in the darkness, mercifully unnoticed in the gas lamp glow. I hadn't really tried to be a gentleman—I was just passing on what I thought was customary—but the compliment she gave me was a very high one. The stated purpose of my Catholic education was for me to become a Catholic Gentleman, and my father always wanted me to be a gentleman—it was the one place where the two worlds connected, family and school. I was embarrassed and elated. I looked at my father. He was beaming a little, too.

The man then said, "How old is your son?"

"He's in the sixth grade, he's eleven."

"I think he could be the youngest person in this line tonight," said our line neighbor. At this I looked up and down the line—we had been joined by a few others at this point—and realized he was right, I was the only kid. I felt very grown up.

"Do you like Eugene Ormandy?"

"This is really my first time to see him in person, but we've got records of his at home—*Peer Gynt* and *Peter and the Wolf*," I responded, thankful that I could remember anything under the pressure of the questioning and my father's proud gaze.

"I think you'll like him in person. He doesn't use a baton, you know, like most of the others."

I nodded wisely at this news, trying to keep an image of formally dressed men twirling rubber-ended silver sticks in a parade, throwing them up and catching them. I knew what she meant, of course, from pictures on the album covers, but I didn't know that the conductor's stick had the same name as the majorette's stick.

I looked beyond our new friends and saw the line filling up, almost reaching back to Broad Street. I turned and looked the other way and was thankful for the position we had.

"What time is it?" I asked my father, trying not to whine about how cold my feet were, trying not to ask "Is it time to go inside yet?" It obviously wasn't, or the line would have been moving.

"It's five minutes after seven, we have less than a half hour to wait. Do you want a cup of cocoa?"

I was surprised by the question. "Sure."

"All right then, wait here, do you folks want anything hot to drink?"—this to the people behind us.

"No, thanks, we're OK, go on, we'll save your place."

"Thanks," he said and off he went, back toward and across Broad Street, weaving between honking taxis. I watched him until he disappeared into a store across the street with a big OPTIMA sign in blinking lights. As I lost sight of him, I had a moment of panic. To calm myself, I began to whistle a tune. "Twinkle, Twinkle, Little Star."

The man in front turned and smiled knowingly, nodding his head in recognition. "Ah, *Eine Kleine Nachtmusik*—Mozart, yah?"

I had no idea what this meant, but I wanted to be a gentleman, so I nodded knowingly back and said "Yah," then mentally kicked myself for imitating the man's accent.

"I'll do the second part," said the man and began to whistle a very complex version of what sounded like "Twinkle, Twinkle, Little Star," only with trills and variations. He could have been a concert whistler.

Conversations up and down the line stopped. People strained to watch my new friend whistling up a storm. I thought of the maple leaves in the wind. The man finished, and a few people applauded. He bowed, comically.

Then he said, "Your turn."

I was at a loss. The first thing that came to my mind was "Oh, What a Beautiful Morning," but I knew that wasn't classical enough for this crew. Then an air from *Peter and the Wolf* popped into my mind, and I wet my lips and started. I didn't have to go long, because the man with the accent picked it up and then, to my amazement, began to walk, or rather dance, to the music, acting out the grandfather. When he had finished, the guy behind me started another tune from the same piece, and before long, there was an entire street performance of *Peter and the Wolf,* which everyone in the line of course knew by heart, people taking turns with the narration and the tunes, some students a few people back pounding on trash cans to make the noise of the hunters.

Our friend with the accent did the complex piccolo part of the bird, and I delivered my favorite line in the piece: "What kind of a bird are *you?*," imitating Cyril Richard's voice from our record at home. The wife of the guy with the accent must have been a dancer, because she was moving gracefully to the duck music when my father came back with the hot chocolate. He stood apart watching the show, winking at me, not wanting to interrupt.

Then the final parade in a circle on the sidewalk outside the Academy of Music: me in the lead, an invisible gun over my shoulder, a wolf with an invisible duck inside, a grandfather who might even have come from the place the music came from. And then it was over, and we were all laughing and shaking hands, and the guy with the accent was telling my father how talented I was, and how I would be a fine musician some day, or perhaps an actor, though that is a hard life. We all got back in line before the doors were opened. I had to gulp down the hot chocolate, but I really didn't need it anymore, warmed as I was by the experience on the sidewalk, and in we went.

My father put down two dollars, picked up two tickets, handed me one, and we started up the stairs.

"It's five flights, Eddie, are you ready, sonny boy?"

"Yes sir, I'm ready. I'll race ya."

"No thanks, Eddie, your father is too old for that."

It then occurred to me that racing up the stairs of the Academy of Music might not be something one was supposed to do, so I went up slowly, taking two steps every now and then to break the monotony. At every other landing there was a window out of which you could see and hear the traffic below, which faded away as we went higher. I was a little surprised that the stairwells were so plain, just cement steps and iron railings; my image of the Academy was much grander.

As we went through the door marked AMPHITHEATRE, however, the true grandness was revealed. Sumptuous maroon rugs met my feet, the fancy stenciled wallpaper met my eyes, and my ears felt the muffling of the sounds of the foot traffic that we were part of. There were wall sconces with flame-shaped lightbulbs dimmed to give a feeling of grand intimacy.

At each door leading to a section of seats there stood a uniformed gentleman with programs, and a helpful, if slightly stuffy, attitude. We didn't need help, though, my father knew just where we were going. He took two programs from the fellow in front of our door, and we walked into a dark balcony and took our seats. I waved to our friends from the street and looked around.

Part of the reason the balcony seemed dark was the bright lights that illuminated the stage far below, set with a hundred or more seats, the last row of which had instruments around it—large bass fiddles, big copper kettledrums, regular drums and racks of percussion instruments, bells, chimes, and triangles. But what was on the stage paled in comparison to the hall itself.

The walls were beautifully papered or painted, around the proscenium arch were statues of muscular figures holding up the ceiling, on which were painted four trios of pagan gods, with spirits of the four seasons interspersed. There were boxes near the stage that seemed to float without support, but the most wondrous thing in the room hung from the middle of the baroquely painted ceiling—a chandelier of about a million crystals that threw rainbows all around from the lights embedded in the structure.

"Trying to catch flies?" asked my father in a bemused voice, waking me from my amazement and informing me, in traditional fashion, that my jaw was hanging down in awe.

"Dad," I whispered, "did you ever see anything like it?"

"The main boiler on the USS *Phoenix* was just as big, though that gave more heat than light, and wasn't nearly as pretty."

I didn't get the joke, transfixed as I was by the glowing object. It seemed to sway just a little bit, though that might have been my imagination, which was soon on to the next issue.

"What if that thing ever fell?" I stood up to see the seats below it, then looked back at the beautiful thing, trying to gauge what percent of the seats would be hit if it did fall. Just about every one.

"It's up there pretty secure, son, don't worry about that."

I sat back down and began to imagine that it would be possible to tie a rope to it and swing from our seats down to the stage. And then I found my hands getting moist as I pictured myself doing that, and then the rope not quite getting to the stage, and me left dangling in midair. I shivered the image off.

"Are you cold, son?"

"No, not at all, its pretty warm in here. Shall we take off our coats."

"Good idea."

Our coats off and folded in our laps, my father asked if I wanted to see the chandelier close up. I said sure, not knowing what he meant. He tapped a box that was connected to the seat in front of me, reached into his pocket, pulled out a quarter, and placed it in the slot. The top of the box flipped up, revealing a small set of binoculars, connected by a wire so it couldn't be taken away except by great force. He handed me the "opera glasses," as he called them, and I looked through. It took a minute to adjust them, but once I managed that the view was very interesting. I could see each crystal of the chandelier, and even reflections of the stage in some of the surfaces. Then my magnified eyes moved along the sides of the balcony and down to the stage, where a few of the musicians were coming in with their instruments, chatting before taking their places to practice passages from the evening's performance.

I handed the glasses to my father and asked, "Do I have time to go to the bathroom?"

"If you go quickly. Want me to come with you?"

"No, I'll be all right, just point me."

He pointed to the far end of the lobby from where we were, and I started over, climbing over our friends from the line, one of whom said: "Going to see a man about a wolf, Peter?"

I nodded and kept on going, pretending to get the joke.

The men's room was big, with an anteroom furnished with chairs and sofas and brass ashtrays. The facilities seemed like antiques—the porcelain of the urinal was crisscrossed with fine hairline cracks, and the plumbing was all brass, with really fancy faucet handles that were like spectacle holders that you moved side to side instead of faucets that you turned.

I tried to find my way back to the seat. I looked in every door, trying to locate my father, finally saw our friends from the line, and navigated the way to my place.

The lights began to dim, and people who were standing and chatting took their seats. The orchestra members ceased their improvisations and practicing.

My father whispered, "Here comes the first oboist to give the *A.*"

I wasn't sure what that meant, but I saw a dignified gentleman enter from the left side of the stage with a brown tube from which extended a smaller pipe. He placed his lips on the pipe, and the sound he made was repeated by all of the other instruments, some of the musicians turning pegs or adjusting mouthpieces, until the *A* was over all. Even the drums were adjusted.

What power that one guy has, I thought, *to get everyone to follow his note.*

Then he sat down. It felt like everyone was holding his breath for what would come next. I certainly was. Then out from the same wing that had produced the oboist came two men with nothing in their hands, and the audience burst into applause. The first man, who had white hair where he had any, gestured to the taller, younger man, who sat down at the gigantic black piano just to the left of the platform which the older man now mounted.

The white-haired man looked around, nodding to some of the people in the orchestra and back to the man at the piano, who nodded back as he held his hands above the keys of the piano. The older man then raised his arms, his hands extending, paused a moment, and raised them for half a second. When he brought them down again, the pianist attacked the keys, the violinists attacked the strings, and we were off. Rachmaninoff's First Piano Concerto.

I looked through the opera glasses and surveyed the swelling scene. Entremont had no sheet music in front of him, he knew his part by heart.

How do you get to the Academy of Music? I rehearsed the old joke in my mind.

Practice, practice, practice.

Or get your father to take you, I thought.

I couldn't believe I was where I was—out with my dad, with strangers friendlier than some of my friends, people with different accents, musicians who knew their work by heart. I felt my eyes welling up with gratitude, and had to use my handkerchief.

"Are you all right?" whispered my dad.

"I'm great, how about you?"

He smiled back. I handed him the opera glasses and sat back for a major flight—over under around and through the chandelier, like a maple leaf blown through prismed rainbows on the winds of Rachmaninoff, there in spirit. But I was there completely.

Coda

At intermission we had orange drink, and I fell asleep during the adagio of the second half but was awake for the final movement. I stood with my father and our new friends and shouted "Bravo!" at the conductor and the soloist.

Then we descended the five flights to Billy Penn and the sea of cabs, and over to the Harvey House for a quick bacon cheeseburger and a Coke, and then back to the car for the ride home.

I fell asleep again to the sound of my father whistling one of the movements. I think I liked his style better than that of the guy with the accent, but I didn't say anything, because I didn't want him to think I loved him too much.

Bonner High, We're Loyal

*T*here was really no question about where I would attend high school. I had gone to Holy Cross for eight years of elementary education, and it was assumed that I would continue my education in the Catholic tradition. There were a couple of options—I could attend one of five expensive Catholic prep schools in the area, or I could go to Monsignor Bonner High, run by the archdiocese and named after a former superintendent.

I took the entrance exam for St. Joseph's Prep School and passed it, but I was not offered the scholarship I would have needed to attend. So it was decided that I would go to Bonner, the school for which Holy Cross was a feeder.

It would cost the family the same as the Upper Darby public high school—nothing. The parish would pay the $150 tuition, thanks to a second collection conducted at Sunday Mass twice a year.

I was very nervous about going. For one thing, it meant that my days of walking to school and coming home for lunch and First Friday breakfast were over. Bonner was three miles away, so walking was not a real possibility, neither for the morning nor for lunch. Holy Cross, however, chartered a school bus for the students who wanted to take it.

A sign of my trepidation came the first morning, when I subconsciously arranged to fall headfirst down the steps on my way to breakfast. I was not hurt enough to miss the first day of school, as some inner demon of mine would have preferred, and I managed to get some breakfast down and board the bus on time.

Although Bonner was an all-boys' school, the sister school, named for Archbishop Prendergast, was located right next door, only a driveway away.

On that first day, the bus arrived and we poured out and entered our respective schools, girls going to Prendergast, boys to Bonner.

As I got out, I looked around at the buildings before me. Although I had passed the site before, I had never been atop the hill that commanded a view of the valley made by a tributary of Darby Creek known as Naylor's Run. You could even see the downtown skyline of the city in the distance, but there was no time for gawking.

The two buildings offered quite a contrast. Prendergast had once been an orphanage built in classical style, dark red brick with cupolas and carriage houses. Bonner had been built practically and plainly, with lighter colored, newer brick. The building was square and low slung, like Holy Cross School had been.

Students were not allowed in the front door until their senior year. We underclassmen entered the side door into a large plain lobby, beyond which was our destination—the auditorium. It was vast. Fifteen hundred wooden seats bolted to the cement floor. On the stage was an altar prepared for the opening

Mass, and a lectern off to one side. We filed in and took our seats next to cards marking the sections we were in.

I had received mail two weeks before assigning me to section D-2. Naturally I thought this meant the second highest class in academic standing, but when I looked around at my classmates, and then back at the other sections, I realized that I was wrong. I had heard on the bus that Michael Kane, smartest kid in eighth grade, was in D-10; as I looked around, it became clear to me that D-2 was not second but that there was another not-so-competetive system that was set up to keep us guessing.

There were a couple of kids from Holy Cross in section D-1, right in front of us, but I knew no one in my section. I tried to comfort myself with the idea that I would be exposed to a whole new group of friends, but that didn't do much to quiet my nerves. I looked around the section trying to identify possible comrades or bullies. Everybody seemed to be pretty nice, on their best behavior for the first day. I was sitting next to a bespectacled Italian kid. I introduced myself, and he said his name was Angelo Falgiani, from St. Alice's Parish.

"Know anything about our homeroom teacher, Father Casey?" I asked.

"A couple of sophomores from my parish said he was an ex-boxer."

"Great," said I, ruminating, "an ex-boxer. I heard he was a little crazy, they call him Wild Bill."

"I heard that too. Do you have him for Religion?" asked Angelo, pulling out his schedule from his coat pocket. We all wore coats and ties, all Catholic Gentlemen. I pulled out my schedule and looked. It read:

HOMEROOM:	*Casey*
WORLD HISTORY:	*Jones*
ALGEBRA I:	*Klemmer*
LUNCH	
ENGLISH:	*Jensen*
LATIN I:	*Casey*
RELIGION:	*Casey*
GENERAL SCIENCE:	*Blake*
GYM:	_____

There was no name listed for Gym, we wouldn't really have it, mostly study halls that freshman year.

"Religion and Latin," I said. "Hope he's not *too* wild, three periods a day could be a little rough with a crazy man."

"Who is also a boxer."

We both laughed nervously.

Just then a priest in a long robe with a simple black cowl and a leather belt took the stage and approached the podium. When he adjusted the microphone, it made a squeaking noise and we all quieted down and looked up.

"Good morning, boys," he said and then he paused, giving us a chance to respond.

"Good morning, Father," we responded, although not in the singsong chant that marked our grade school days.

The kid in front of me, however, said, "Good morning, priest," just loud enough for a few of us to hear, slumping down into the seat from whence he could crack wisely ad libitum. His name was Sharkey, I would find out later, and his willing audience sitting next to him was Schank. They were both from the same parish and obviously had a rapport which would later prove deadly to some of the teachers during the year. They would sit in front of me in the row near the window, the privilege of the S's, T's, and V's.

"Welcome to Monsignor Bonner High School. I'm Father Kennedy, the principal. Your parishes are all paying good money for your education here, and I want you all to work hard and make your parents proud of you. I'm going to ask the Student Guards now to pass out your handbooks, and I'll go over a few of the rules so you'll know exactly what is expected of you."

The phrase *Student Guards* had a strange tone to it, and I half-expected some kind of crew with uniforms and perhaps swords or guns. A group of rather large seniors with green armbands that said STUDENT GUARD on them came up the aisle and started passing out little white books with the school seal on the cover. One of them punched a kid sitting by the aisle as he passed them out.

Angelo leaned over and whispered, "That's his brother, Frankie Carr, they're in my parish."

I noticed a resemblance, same burr haircut, same stocky look.

Angelo continued, "Football." Ah, that explained it. The older Carr was actually a star on the Bonner team, the younger would play on the freshman team, in the shadow of his more able brother. I was glad there were no older Stivenders with reputations to contend with.

"Boys," continued the priest when we all had a copy, "in this little booklet are all the rules for success at Bonner High School. Make sure you read it tonight. Meanwhile, I'd like to point out a few important parts. Turn to page thirteen."

We did so, and read along with Father: "There is to be no congregating with any students from Prendergast High School at the trolley stops or bus stops around the school grounds or on the school grounds itself." Looking up, he said, "This is a very important rule. Read along with me: There is to be no smoking while in uniform within three blocks of the school."

He looked up again. "The reason for this should be obvious, we don't want to give scandal to our neighbors. And we don't want anyone here to be confused with the smokers from Upper Darby or Beverly Hills"—the two public schools nearby, one located at the edge of the archdiocesan property.

"Being a student at Bonner is a privilege, not a right, and it can be taken away from you at any time, so obey the rules and you'll stay in school." The obvious catchiness of this rhyme was lost on the speaker, I think, who had given the same speech many times over the past five years.

"Are there any questions?" No one moved, except Sharkey shifting in the silence. "Very well, we'll begin our Mass."

It would be the first time I saw altar boys without cassock and surplice, dressed just like the rest of us, serving at the portable altar. We'd learn later that they were members of the Bonner Breakfast Club, whose main duty it was to assist the priests at Mass every morning in the Augustinian monastery behind the school. It would be my first high school club.

The Mass completed, Father Kennedy took the podium again and dismissed us by section to the halls where we would look for our homerooms. The students in D-2 were to report to Room 2, on the ground floor. Walking down the corridors for the first time was quite a shock—seemingly infinite hallways lined on both sides with steel lockers painted gray, skinny ones, with little closets above, two together.

The school had just been cleaned, as I could tell from the smell and the way the shiny floors squeaked underfoot as we searched for Room 2. Finally finding it, we filed in and sat down. Whereas the desks at Holy Cross were wooden and cast-iron-filigree affairs bolted to runners in fixed rows, the desks at Bonner were free-standing, individual ones, with the writing surface extending from the back of the seat and buttressed by metal rods from the seat itself. The wooden surfaces were etched with names and drawings that had been sanded down and shellacked over, with little success. The desk that I was sitting in had been manned by "Jeff/58" and some others who were illegible now. There was a trace of the figure of Kilroy, nose and hands below the line representing a wall, big eyes rising above it. There were also a few holes drilled with a compass point or ballpoint pen.

Beneath the seat was a space for books and lunch. No books yet, no lunch either, since today was a half-day. Although we were unsupervised, there was no fooling around. As freshmen, we still had the customary awe and fear.

Suddenly the door opened and slammed. In glided a short round-headed, balding, red-haired man in a long cassock but without a cowl; this gave us the immediate information that he was not an Augustinian but a secular priest (thereby making him slightly more dangerous). He flashed onto the riser in the front of the room that held his desk, banged his leather over-stuffed bookbag on the surface of it, placed his knuckle on either side of it, leaned over and glared at us, with a slight smile full of strength creeping across his face. What he lacked in height, he made up for in stock, the cassock tight around his chest and arms, wide with muscle, not fat. He demanded respect by his very presence. That morning, we gladly gave it to him.

"I'm your homeroom teacher, Father Casey, and you are section D-Two, anybody here not supposed to be here?" His eyes searched the room, most of us holding our breath.

"I will now read the seat assignments in alphabetical order." He reached into his overstuffed bag and produced a chart which he began to read quickly. "First seat first row, Basilio, behind him Brown, behind him Burke ..."

No one had moved. He looked up and raised his eyebrows.

"All cripples, eh? Do I have to pick up each one of you?" He pointed to a kid in the first seat, first row. "Are you Basilio?"

"No, Father, Quinn," said the kid in a shaky voice.

"Why are you sitting in Basilio's seat? Do your feet work?"

"Yes, Father."

"Then work them, boy. Basilio, where are you?"

A hand went up in the third row.

"Need help getting to your seat?"

"No, Father."

Basilio started toward his seat, and Casey went back to his chart "... behind Basilio, Brown, behind Brown, Burke."

Now forty-three boys were falling over desks and each other as they tried to keep up with Casey's quick pace. I made for the window aisle, relinquishing my seat to two guys at once in this odd game of musical chairs. They discussed the matter, giving each other their names and figuring it out. All over the room there were conferences as kids tried to get close to their actual seats. Wisely, I waited as he got to the last row.

"Schank, first seat last row, Sharkey behind him, Stapleton behind him, Stivender behind him ..."

The first moment of crisis had passed—he pronounced my name right, with a long *i*.

"... Stott behind him, Sykes behind him, Totaro, Vail, Vitali."

He looked up from his chart to see a few disputes in the next-to-last row. In the silence that followed, they were settled quickly and quietly. Then everybody was seated, hands on their desks. *He may not be really crazy, but he's good,* I thought. He had us jumping.

He looked at us, lips pursed almost to a smile, eyebrows raised. "Everybody where they should be? Good. That's where you'll sit when you come to homeroom every day. Anybody not like their seat?"

Even though we all knew this was a rhetorical question, I almost raised my hand. Room 2 was in the basement of the school, so the windows were high and didn't start until Charlie Stott's seat, behind me. I wouldn't be able to daydream out the window as much as I had grown used to in grade school.

But I knew this was no time to discuss it. I did raise my hand, though, because my case of nerves had reached my lower tract and my hands were sweating. The runs!

Casey knew I was sick when he looked at me.

"Are you sick, Stivender? Put your head down on the desk."

"Actually Father, I think I better be excused."

"All right, the bathroom's down the hall to the right."

I ran, and luckily I made it into the cool tiled bathroom with more stalls than I had ever seen in one room, and did what I had to do, almost fainting as I sat but making it in time.

Oh, great, I thought to myself, *first day and I'm sick in front of all the kids in my homeroom. They're gonna think I'm a fairy.*

I returned sheepishly to the room and took my seat. Casey spared me the attention that would surely have sealed my doom and didn't stop speaking when I came in. He was talking about discipline.

"Now boys, you all know what detention is, but in this class we have a special punishment, in fact two special punishments, the Green Bench and the You Got It. If I say to you during homeroom or any of the classes we might have together, 'You got it,' that means you have to turn in a composition of two hundred fifty words for each You Got It you get, on the Bible passage cited on the board over there."

He pointed to the far corner of the blackboard where, in a little drawn square were the words *Matthew 1:1–2:4.*

"You go home that night and read the passage from scripture and paraphrase it in your own two hundred fifty words, or five hundred, or seven fifty, et cetera. If you miss turning it in, you get double. Understood?"

We all nodded silently.

"The Green Bench is something else entirely. It's the invisible bench all along the back wall. Turn around and look."

We did so. The wall was green, and the bench was indeed invisible.

"If you get caught doing something foolish, I will ask you to sit on the Green Bench until you learn better. But I'm sure none of you will ever have to go there. It's not much fun."

We would soon discover that the knees gave out after a few minutes.

"Now, one thing that you will surely get a You Got It for is sneezing without covering your mouth. Let me show you what happens when you do that."

He took a piece of chalk and approached the slate blackboard that covered the front wall. There he drew a profile of a face with a nose, eyes, and an open mouth.

"Inside each one of us is the miracle of life. Part of the miracle of life is the mystery of germs." He drew a series of dots where the throat of the profiled figure would be. "Each of us has our own germs, some are good, some are bad. In this class, you want to keep your germs to yourself. You don't want to share these germs with anyone in the room. Sometimes you may want to sneeze. What happens to the germs when you sneeze without covering your mouth and nose?"

Here he started rapping dots on the board in front of the profile, filling the board with a chalk-storm. "Germs, boys, germs, filling the world with your germs. Do that and You Got It. Get it?"

We all nodded.

"Good."

His health was obviously important to Father Casey and he was going to protect it with disciplinary measures.

"All right, the next order of business is locker keys. Basilio, here is a list with everyone's name on it. I'll give one of these envelopes with a key in it to each boy and call out the number, you put the number in the little nicktuflaterberotum next to it."

This was the first time we would hear what would turn out to be Casey's trademark, double-talk words that sounded slightly scientific yet made no sense, but which everyone knew the meaning of because of the context. The balance between sternness and humor was Casey's secret. He would be a beloved teacher by most that came into contact with him, except for the few foolish enough to really cross him.

"Then," he continued, "each of you is to go out into the corridor, find your locker and try the key to make sure it works. Basilio, A-Five."

Basilio put the number in the space next to his name.

"You'll try yours last, Basilio. Burke, A-Six."

Burke took the envelope from the priest and left the room, and so on and so forth until:

"Stivender, A-Forty-five."

I walked up to Casey, still a little weak in the knees, took the envelope, and walked out to find the locker.

Both walls of the corridor were lined with the skinniest lockers imaginable, each with a book storage compartment above it, which was connected with an interior rod to one of the two lockers below, so the book compartment was twice as wide as the coat section. Later on in the year, we would learn the trick of opening the top section with the heel of a shoe when we forgot our key, but now I just wondered at the dents in the knob of the upper compartment. With a little jiggle, the key worked fine, and I returned to my seat in the classroom. No problem. I was feeling a little better, physically.

"All right, boys, we have a really short schedule today, since it's only a half-day. So now it's almost time to change classes and go to your first period. When the bell rings, move quickly and quietly to the next class."

When the bell finally rang, we all got up and left. Just outside the door, however, I felt someone punch me, hard, in the upper arm. I looked for the source of this injustice and saw the brother of the Student Guard glaring at me with an odd glint in his eye. Frankie Carr. He didn't say anything, just turned and walked down the hall. My new friend Angelo saw the whole thing.

"Welcome to high school," was all he said.

Finding my way around the school that day was a little bit difficult at first, but once I learned which stairwells went up and which went down, and that the cafeteria was directly under the gym, and so forth, things got easier. I also got a chance to see what the Student Guards did. They seemed to be all football players or student council types, and their main task was to stand in the hallways and keep the traffic moving around them.

That first day I learned a few of the unwritten rules of the school. I refused several sales of elevator passes from sopho-mores (there were no elevators in the school) and had a chance to partake in the age-old custom of carrying upperclassmen's books. My bowels still nervous and my arm still hurting from the punch, I went through the day with as much good humor as I could muster, thankful for the new friendships with Angelo and Charlie Stott, who sat behind me in most of my classes.

From Casey's homeroom most of us went to Mr. Jones's World History class. Almost all of our teachers were young, and Jones was no exception. With his herringbone jackets and horn-rimmed glasses, he really looked like a teacher. He was balding on the top of his head and spent most of the time walking up and down the aisles of the class lecturing on history, stopping momentarily to rap certain ones of us with his large college ring. This was his major skill, it seemed, and he could do it without missing a beat in his sentence, though often we missed a word if the victim responded vocally to the pain. Sometimes it was hard to know why he was hitting us, since we rarely acted up when he was walking in our row, and the distance in time between the infraction and the strike was often great.

"And so, boys, the Greek *[strike]* invention of the city–state, the democracies that were *[strike]* developed because of it, and the inter-city-state alliances *[strike]* enabled culture to develop most quickly around the Aegean *[strike]* Sea." Every so often he would pause at the end of a row, reach into his pocket and produce a handkerchief and wipe his glasses. Without these breaking up his face he looked vulnerable, but he could see without them, as some of us found out.

Our second period brought us to Father Klemmer, one of the gifts of the Louvain. This venerable university in Belgium must have been a stronghold of the Augustinian order in Europe, for we would have several of her graduates, all with the same indecipherable accent. They sounded like there was wadding just beyond their tonsils that kept the vowels from coming out clearly, and when they did come out, they came out their nose. This aspect of Father Klemmer's visage was bountiful, his profile similar to those on ancient Roman coins.

He also had the distinctly European—or so we thought—custom of avoiding deodorant. His accent made him fair game as well; his vulnerability as a foreigner made him easy prey to Sharkey and some of the other wise guys in the class. But he was a good algebra teacher, I think. I can still do binomial operations.

After Algebra it was time for lunch. On this, the first day, we weren't served food, but we marched in anyway for practice. Third-period lunch began, on a normal day, at 10:28, a little early for my system, but we all got used to it. Early lunch was necessitated by the number of kids who had to use the cafeteria each day. There were some three thousand of us, after all, in the school, in my class alone almost a thousand. We were the Baby Boom.

The cafeteria itself was the same size as the gym. It was vast, with long cast-iron-based tables with green asphalt linoleum surfaces and round uncomfortable stool-tops that swung out on cast-iron arms from below. Designed more for efficiency of cleaning than comfort, these seats were hard enough when you sat upon them facing the table; they were even more uncomfortable with your back against the table edge as you sat at detention after school. Almost as uncomfortable as Casey's Green Bench.

For eight years I had had the luxury of eating lunch at home, in easy walking distance from the school. Now I would have to start bringing my lunch. For ten cents you could buy a grape or orange juice, and for the same price a piece of layer cake or two pretzels. Cokes and other carbonated beverages were not available. (I used to think they were too decadent for a Catholic school. Now I suspect it had something to do with the efficacy of carbonated beverages in a food fight, of which there were very few, at least at third period.) If you didn't bring your lunch you could buy a boiled hot dog for a dime, but only a fool used the mustard, which sat out in bowls with brushes, open to the expectoration of the upperclassmen, who went through the line ahead of us freshmen.

After lunch period, we had English, another Augustinian, Father Jensen. A classic jock, he was probably born to be a coach, and his classes were full of odd ruminations about sports topics of which I knew little and for which I cared not at all. Every Friday he gave the same composition assignment— go to Bonner's football game on Sunday and write about it. At this time in Philadelphia there was a brilliant sportswriter by the name of Sandy Grady who was this guy's hero, and sometimes he would read his column aloud and expect the same style from us. But this was not my idea of a good time with the English language. I was not a sports fan.

Luckily I had Casey's Latin class that year, in which I learned more about my mother tongue than in Jensen's class. It came right after English, and I always arrived ready for rules of grammar and syntax, so the timing was good that way.

I enjoyed Wild Bill a lot. He was a vibrant teacher, always moving around the room with chalk and sometimes an eraser in his hand, talking very fast, sometimes in English, sometimes in Latin, sometimes in his original brand of gibberish. He had eyes not only in the back of his head, but all over, and if your attention lagged, or you were fooling around, he would throw the eraser with remarkable accuracy and speed, assigning You Got Its with aplomb.

Having him for two classes a day was no problem, either, since he was following two different syllabi. On that first day, in Religion class, he used visual aids of a new sort. He started out by asking an old question about God from the catechism: "Where is God?"

We all knew the answer: "God is everywhere." It looked like a humdrum exercise in review, when all of a sudden, he ran down the third aisle, swept a kid out of his seat, sped him to the back of the room, shoved him into the closet, and closed the door.

He certainly knew how to get our attention. My original thought was that the kid had done something wrong and this was a punishment, perhaps the Green Closet to match the Bench. But when he started asking him questions, it became clear it was part of the lesson.

"Can you see anything in there?" he asked, leaning up against the door to make sure the kid heard him.

The muffled voice: "No."

"All right then, can you see yourself?"

(Muffled) "No."

"Can you see God?"

"No."

"Is God in there?"

Obviously a trick question. There was a long pause.

"Hello, are you still in there?" Casey yelled.

We laughed. Casey's signal quieted us quickly.

"I didn't hear you, what did you say?"

(Muffled, but obviously in an attempt to be louder, now with a slight tinge of panic) "I'm still here."

"Good, I thought you might have escaped through the quartereetizone"—this would be Casey's favorite word, it could mean almost anything—"So you're still in there, right?"

"Right."

"Can you see your hand?"

"No," came the voice a little weakly.

Casey, sensing panic, opened the door. "Are you all right?"

"Yes." Blinking.

Casey, satisfied that he was, closed the door on him and said, "Let's begin again."

"Can you see anything?"

(Stronger) "No."

"Can you see your hand?"

"No."

"Your feet?"

"No."

"Where is God?"

"God is everywhere."

"Is God in there."

A pause. "Yes."

"Can you see Him?"

"No."

"Can you see yourself?"

"No."

"Are you in there?"

"Yes."

"How do you know?"

"I can feel myself."

The double entendre took a half-second to sink in, and we began to laugh.

Casey opened the door. "Oh, no you don't, not in my closet."

The kid was liberated, laughing weakly, and sat down to pats on the back from his mates.

Casey continued, "OK, boys, this little demonstration shows us one thing: we can't always say how we know a thing is true, and truth goes beyond the senses, into the realm of Faith. We'll be looking at Faith and the Bible this year, and there may be some difficult questions we'll discuss, but you won't be in the dark for long, and even in the dark, you'll see things clearly."

Then the bell rang. Casey had the timing of a boxer, that's for sure.

Our last class of the day was General Science with Mr. Blake. The problem with Mr. Blake is that he didn't notice if we were in the room with him or not. He seemed to prefer talking to the ceiling or the lights hanging from it or the clouds outside the window, to talking to us. If we happened to be there to collect his wisdom, all well and good, if not, more's the pity, but it didn't really matter. We didn't know what to make of him. He wouldn't have known what to make of us, if he had ever condescended to notice our presence. He would speak in long sentences, his jaw thrust as though he were very tough or on the verge of tears, or perhaps both. He lived with his mother and had flunked out of seminary, at least that was the rumor. He wouldn't last the year, but that's another story.

After the classes were over, we stood in line to buy our books. This was another aspect of high school that would be different from grade school, where the books were provided by the archdiocese, kept carefully covered through the school year, then returned to the boxes in the closet for use by the next year's class. At Bonner, we would buy our books new each year, unless we knew a kid in the grade ahead of us, which I did not. It was an expensive proposition, these books, and I'm not sure where the money came from, but I had enough to buy them. I suspect my mother went without some things she could have used, but I was never made aware of it. I put most of my books in my locker and headed home, troubled a little about the contact with the bully in my class, not sure what to do about it.

No one was home when I got there. My mother had taken a job at the local department store, and my sisters were still in school. After changing into my after-school clothes, I went down to the basement to my comic book collection. I had two types of comics, *Classics Illustrated,* cartoon versions of literature, and regular comics.

I opened one of my *Supermans* to the inside cover where I saw my plight with Carr clearly illustrated. At the top of the page was the photo of the Muscle Man, Charles Atlas, in a body-building pose, and in the middle of the page there was a line drawing showing a ninety-seven-pound weakling getting sand kicked in his face by a muscular man on the beach. The next panel showed the big guy stealing the little guy's girlfriend and laughing. There it was, me and Frankie Carr, although there was no girl in the real life story I was leading.

At my pre-entrance physical, Dr. Scally had weighed me. Exactly ninety-seven pounds. I was the guy in the picture, and Charles Atlas had a solution for me. I retrieved a dollar from my sock drawer and sent off for the introductory offer. It would be a few weeks before I received any magical solutions from him, so I decided to talk to my father about it.

After dinner I did.

"Dad, what do you know about bullies?" I asked as objectively as I could, not wanting him to know there was a particular bully that I needed to deal with.

"Some one at school bothering you?"

"Who, me? Oh no, it's for an English assignment."

"Oh, I see." If he didn't believe me, he didn't show it. "Well, one thing I know for sure is, I always feel sorry for them. There was a kid at the orphanage that always picked on the weaker kids, and we all knew that he had a rough time before coming to us, all bruised and battered. Apparently his father beat him all the time, social workers finally had to take him away from his parents and gave him to us. It was like he was trying to make up for all the pain he had had." I thought of the scene that morning with the older brother. "After a while, though, once he realized he wasn't going to get beat, he calmed down and became friendly. He just needed time."

Maybe that's all Carr needed, time.

The next day he was waiting for me, right inside the homeroom door. *Wham.*

I looked at him and rubbed my arm. "Minimum daily requirement," he said.

My plan was to get on the Charles Atlas program, gain some weight, get some muscles, and then call him out for a fight down under the trestle. This was a very high wooden bridge that took the trolley over the Naylor's Run waterway. It was just beyond school property and out of sight of the Augies.

And so every day I had to put up with this ignominy. I wasn't sure whether he meant it was *his* daily requirement to hit me, or *my* daily requirement to be hit. Either way, it went on.

Finally, in the third week of school, I found a package waiting for me from the mailman when I got home one day. The return address was Charles Atlas! Here was the solution to my problem, I hoped.

I don't know what I expected, but when I got down to my private place in the basement and opened the package I was very disappointed. It was just a booklet with pictures and descriptions of exercises—exercises I already knew about, although I had never thought of using telephone books or buckets of water to do them. Basically, the book had helpful hints about using household items for weights. The problem was that they would take time. Lots of time. And concentration. Throughout the booklet were motivational statements from Charles next to pictures of posing musclemen, mostly him, but none of it seemed too exciting or inviting.

I tried them out for a few days until I reached the conclusion that would doom my regimen of body-building forever. It was boring. Body-building was boring. My attention span for Latin, Algebra, and History was quite good, but for this it was nonexistent. I put the booklet with the rest of my comics and gave up that aspect of the game. Taking Frankie Carr out physically was not going to be an option for me after all.

My problem with the bully was resolved quite differently than I had expected, and at first I didn't even realize it had happened. What was supposed to happen, of course, was that I would confront him and hit him in the nose and send him crying to the nurse's office, like the big baby that he was inside, but that wasn't in the cards.

It happened in History class. Jones was walking up and down the aisles talking about the Founding Fathers, when he came upon a name we were supposed to know about.

"And, now, who can tell me about John Jay?"

Suddenly, out of my mouth, with little control from me, came the words, "John Jay who?" Meaning, John J. who.

Why this was particularly funny that day, I'm not sure— whether it was Jones's pomposity, or the nervousness that came from most of the class not doing the reading the night before, or what—but the class in one voice laughed aloud, including Frankie Carr.

Jones's face turned red. He took off his glasses to wipe them and, focusing on his cleaning, he said, "All right, who is the wise guy?"

Everyone fell silent. He must have thought it came from Sharkey, two seats ahead of me, because he looked over at him. Sharkey shook his head with a mixture of defensiveness and jealousy because of the laugh it got, and Jones knew he wasn't the one.

"Well?"

It would have been easy for my classmates to give me away with just a look, but no one did. All of a sudden I had power that I never had before. It wasn't physical power, but some kind of social power. I'm not sure where it came from. Later on,

Jones would talk about the social contract implicit in all government where the people assent to the power given to a king or parliament. I wouldn't clearly see the connection, but this day I felt it. Now all I had to do was keep a straight face. Which of course, I couldn't do. And so Mr. Jones knew, and made his way toward me, my head in one hand trying to hide my laughter.

"Mr. Stivender, eh? Our new class clown, eh? John Jay who, indeed."

He was making his way toward me menacingly, his college ring glistening in the florescent glare of the lights, as he raised it to strike.

"Wouldn't it be *whom?* John Jay *whom?*" With each *whom* came a shot of his ring on the crown of my head. I was surprised how much it really hurt, but not as much as Carr's fist on my arm. For at least here was an element of just deserts, I was being punished for something I did, not for who—or whom—I was.

Recovering, Jones continued his line of inquiry. "Who can tell me who John Jay was?"

Luckily, Angelo Falgiani knew. He raised his hand, and the moment passed as Jones called on him and went on with his lecture.

The next day Frankie Carr was just inside the door of the homeroom with his fist, but he didn't use it on me. Nor the next day or the next. Somehow I had won his respect, and perhaps his fear. As I became better and better in my role as class clown, I gained greater social classroom power. Carr didn't want to mess with a guy who could verbally take on all his teachers—all except Casey, whose sense of timing was the only one better than mine. Wild Bill had been a boxer, after all.

Mr. Browne, with an e

*T*here were several "tracks" at Bonner. The high IQ boys were in the honors track, below that was the scientific track, then came the commercial track (the main new skill in this one being mechanical drawing), and finally there ran the general track, meaning the boys who had gotten the short end of this triage. Little was expected of them.

I was placed in the scientific track, which would mean that I would be offered a science every year—Biology in the tenth grade, Chemistry in eleventh grade (though I took the Latin III option instead), and Physics in twelfth.

In my freshman year, I had General Science. Our assigned teacher was Mr. Blake. He was a big man but not fat, with a great square face, thrust jaw, and wide shoulders. Although his presence was imposing, he had a faraway look in his eye—a habit of talking with his eyes focused over our heads—and a hint of sadness that we could never quite define.

The story was that he lived with his mother, within walking distance of the school, and had once been in the seminary. His credentials in the yearbook list his bachelor's degree as being from St. Charles Borromeo, the Diocesan Seminary of Philadelphia.

He had dropped out before ordination, apparently, and there were several stories of explanation: the gentler ones had to do with taking care of his mother, the less respectful stories had him flunking out, because he couldn't take the regimen.

Although I had accepted the mantle of class clown from my classmates early that year, I never plied this trade at Blake's expense, as did some of the bolder fellows like Jim Sharkey. To me, Blake wasn't much of a challenge, because he really didn't get it. His feet were too far off the ground for him to notice there was clowning going on around him, and it's no real sport of there isn't a chance of getting caught, in my opinion. Besides, I was a little bit in awe of him. He was the only lay teacher who admitted to saying a daily rosary, as I tried to do.

Furthermore, I enjoyed the subject matter. I had been a member of the parish Science Club in grade school. We met on Saturday mornings, and our leaders were a couple of fathers who were scientists themselves—some sort of engineers, I think. My favorite project in Science Club was the turbine I made out of an old paint can and the top of a frozen orange juice can that I punched, cut, and bent to make a wheel that, when placed just so on a bent paper-clip axle, would whirl from the steam forced out of a small hole in the top of the can filled with water, set on a hot stove. It was a project one couldn't do at home because we didn't have the tools there, or the design.

We didn't have lab in General Science, though there were little experiments you could perform at home. Mostly the class had to do with simple physics. I enjoyed it in spite of Blake's strange bearing.

One day in February of my freshman year, when we should have all stayed home, we strayed from the material in the textbook. It had been snowing, the kind of late winter wet snow that weighs down the trees and slushes up the roads, but doesn't offer too many prospects for sledding or snowman building. He was staring out the window as we filed in for class, and when the bell rang he came out of his reverie long enough to recognize that he was not alone.

"Well, boys, quite a day, quite a day. Take out your homework from last night and put it on your desks, I'll come around and look at it."

He walked around with his mark book, putting a check beside the names of the boys who had their homework, and a different mark for those who did not. When he was finished, he took his place at his desk and continued to stare out the window.

"The snow, boys, the snow, covering all the earth and all its sins. It's Our Lady's snow, boys, Our Lady's snow, each flake is a crystal rosary bead, the earth is saying her rosary with the snow. Our Lady's chaplet, it is, each flake a bead, and every tree a cross. 'Loveliest of trees, the cherry now / Is hung with snow along the bough,' as the poet says."

We shifted in our seats. We were beginning to suspect something was a little wrong. We looked at each other nervously, but none of the class, not even Sharkey, bravest of our clown crew, was making any wisecracks. It occurred to me that Blake was making a kind of breakthrough, telling us directly what he was always thinking.

He got up and walked over to the window. The room had a great view of the lawn that separated the school from the girls' high school across the way. It was one of the three rooms that offered a spectacular view when the girls were having fire drills. But there were none today, just the lawn, the snow, and one lone tree that had been planted just a few years ago in honor of someone or other. Just a sapling, really.

Blake stared at it. "And the one solitary tree in all the snow, it is a tree like the tree of Calvary, boys, like Calvary, and there's the Blessed Mother, standing at the foot of the cross."

I wasn't really disturbed by this thought—my imagination could take such things seriously, like shapes in clouds, for instance—though I did get out of my seat just a nudge to see if there was anything unusual going on outside. Nothing. The unusual was happening on the inside. Inside Blake's mind.

"The foot of the Cross, the foot of the Cross," he mumbled and lowered his head. There were tears in his eyes, and I was praying that none would fall. Having a teacher cry in the classroom would have broken a code of implicit trust that male teachers had with their male students—in 1960, anyway.

He composed himself somewhat and went back to his seat, saying "This is a great day for Our Lady, boys, a great day, Our Lady of the Snow." He looked at us distractedly, then said, "Take out your notebooks and write an essay on sublimation of H_2O from ice to vapor for the rest of the period." Then, while we nervously obeyed, he looked out the window until the bell rang, releasing us to final class of the day.

We had study hall in place of General Science the rest of the week, and on Monday, a new teacher sat at the desk when we filed in. On the blackboard was written the name *Mr. Browne.* He was thin and had curly hair and a high forehead. His clothes looked older than he was, and tweedy; his tie was skinnier than the rest of the teachers, as though he had been out of the country for a while and missed a few years of subtle trends.

He rose from his seat and walked across the room to close the door as soon as the bell rang. Then he paused dramatically, scanning the room with his frowning eyes. He walked back to the board, pointing at it and saying, "With an *e* boys, with an *e*, my name is Browne, with an *e*. I graduated from St. Michael's College at the University of Toronto, my degree is in Philosophy, and I have come to replace Mr. Blake, who had to go in the hospital. He won't be back this year, so I will be your General Science teacher."

He spoke articulately, but with a slight accent that I couldn't place, perhaps Canadian. He didn't look above our heads, but I sensed an air of disdain. He knew he was smarter than us, and wanted us to know it too. Being smarter than us would be his whip, his disciplinary tool. And it worked—on two levels. It made us afraid of him and, for me, set up a great challenge—if not to be as smart as him, to get noticed by him as smart, or at least witty.

I knew somehow that I could not use my normal tack with a guy like Browne, couldn't place a well-timed barb or wise-crack at his expense. I had to wait for a more suitable time. It came during a lesson on magnetism. We were just starting the chapter on electricity, the longest one in the book, and we were learning the elements that could be magnetized and spun through coils to make an electric charge. He was talking about a book on the subject that he had found in a room down the hall, the library.

He always referred to our school library as that "shelf of books" as a way to distinguish it from a real library, like the one at his alma mater. On this particular day he had used the word *magnificent* to refer to it, and this surprised us.

He knew from our looks that we had missed the point, again. So he said, "I was using irony."

The blank or confused looks must have continued, because he gave an exasperated sigh and said, "All right, who can tell us what *irony* means."

Finally, my chance was clear. I raised my hand, the only one visible above fifty consternated faces. I of course knew what irony was, had used it myself a time or two in my life, but the proximity to the lesson we were studying created an opening I could not pass up.

He looked at the seating chart on his desk. "Mr. Stivender?"

"Irony, having the quality or attribute of iron," I said in as straight a face as I could muster. And for one split second, I knew I had him.

He blinked, in the face-down sense of the word. His guard of superiority was lowered for a half-second as he frowned at my answer, and a half-second later, when he realized the excellence of my thrust, the slightest smile wafted over his face. It was a moment just between us, and then he was back to his public self, in control, as he said:

"Mr. Stivender has made a little witticism, and has used a little irony himself in rendering this clever definition to our discussion."

There, he used the word *clever*. I had succeeded in my attempt: he had noticed me. After that day, I became one of his eyeholds in the class, a person to whom he would look when making a point, or giving a lesson, and he referred to the irony comment several times during that year.

Part of the reason that I liked him was the fact that his chin was not pronounced in the same way that mine was not, and we were of the same body type. He became my first real role model for what I would like to be like when I grew up. He was the first layman to play the priest's role of replacing my father.

My father was a Navy man. He had served in the Pacific in the '40s and in Korea in the '50s, and whenever he began to feel constrained by the requirements of land, he would re-up for another stint. He was gone these days, and I was in need of a substitute. One brilliant social feature of the Catholic church and the celibate priesthood is every priest's availability for surrogation. The widows and old ladies see the priest as an ideal son; kids like me, temporarily or permanently without a father, see him as a surrogate father. I had already done so with Father

Casey a little bit, but here was a guy, a single guy, not a priest, who could perform a similar service to my imagination. But how to get closer to him? There was only one real way: get in trouble and have to stay after school in his classroom.

Part of Browne's condescending stance toward the Augustinian administration was the holding of his own detention, instead of sending the culprit to the general detention in the cafeteria. I don't think I was begging for attention, but I was glad when an incident occurred that resulted in my staying after school.

Water pistols are of course contraband in almost any Catholic school setting, except perhaps the last day of school, or a special dispensation day. It was neither of these the day I brought a small red twenty-nine-cent jobber into the classroom and shot John Schank two seats up, whose response caused a disturbance and stopped Browne in the middle of a sentence.

Browne turned slowly to look at the culprit who interrupted him with the outburst. Schank was wiping the back of his head. Browne knew exactly what was going on and scanned the row back through the line of fire to see my reddening face looking down at my desk, one hand in my coat pocket.

"Mr. Stivender! Please stand up," he said as he made his way toward me across the room. At the time I was sitting in the first row, seventh seat down, so I had time to pass it to the kid behind me as I stood, who then passed it further on surreptitiously and efficiently. By the time Browne was on me, the pistol had disappeared.

"Stand up," said Browne in an angry voice.

I stood.

"Give me the water pistol."

"I don't have a water pistol," I said; in truth, I did not.

"Hand out of your pocket."

I obeyed, nothing in my hand.

"Empty your coat pockets," he said, knowing it would not be in my pants pocket where it could have leaked and caused embarrassment.

Onto the desk I placed my rosary in its plastic case, three pens and two pencils, several pieces of folded paper, as well as coupons from wrappers of Mallo Cups—my favorite candy—in dollar amounts. When you had five dollars' worth, you could send them in and get a whole box of Mallo Cups.

The paper was wet. I was caught wet-handed.

"I don't have time for this, you'll stay after school every day for two weeks and copy the chapter on electricity in longhand. If you're finished in less than two weeks, you will end your detention."

I sat down scowling for the benefit of my friends. I felt a little guilty for trying to trick my mentor but mostly glad that I had been condemned to the fate of keeping Browne company as he marked his papers and did other homework at his desk after school. For the first several days, we worked in punishment mode, me sulkily, silently writing out the work in longhand, learning more about electricity than I would ever care to know. One direct result of this exercise was high marks on the tests for that unit.

Browne would sit at his desk working, me watching him out of the corner of my eye, while doing my work. Every so often he would lean back in his chair and put his feet up on the desk and stare out the window. Although it was a little hard to imagine, he looked like he was daydreaming, my favorite thing to do. This made me like him even more.

One day, when he was in this position, he deigned to speak. "Not very nice weather, eh?" It had rained earlier in the day, it was just drizzle now.

"Hmmmm," I grunted in agreement.

"How many pages to go?"

"About seven." I was actually halfway through, but I wanted to sound appropriately overburdened.

"Ah, Mr. Stivender, this too will pass, this too will pass." These words would be like a verbal amulet that I would keep hidden in my heart all through my adolescence; whenever I was in a rough place, in trouble, or depressed, I could hear Browne's voice. I would learn later that he was quoting an Old English lay.

Trying to get the attention off myself, I asked, "Is it still raining?"

"Actually it seems to be escaping the Aristotelian principle of identity."

I had heard of Aristotle. Browne had mentioned his name several times during class. He was a philosopher that Browne had studied at St. Mike's, that much I knew.

I took the bait. "The Aristotelian principle of identity?"

"Yes, I'm sure you know it: a thing cannot be both A and non-A at the same time."

Of course I had not heard it before, and I didn't know what it meant now that I had. But the possibility of an actual conversation with this man on a topic not in the book was too exciting to let go. So I struggled, using the same mental muscles that I exercised in making wisecracks, trying to make connections. After a few seconds I said warily:

"Then, it cannot be both raining and not raining at the same time."

It still didn't make complete sense, but somewhere in my brain a light was glowing—or if not a light, a tool of thinking was being set into place. A Rule of Being was being offered to me, and I was almost grasping it.

"Very good, Mr. Stivender, you are as quick today as you were on Monday, though in a different mode of discourse from sneaking in water pistols."

"Yes, sir," I said, putting my head and hand back to work.

Although it did occur to me to slow down my writing to take the full two weeks of detention, I was finished by Monday of the second week. As the year progressed, however, I took the liberty of stopping by his classroom just to chat now and then. I no longer needed him as a surrogate father. But I will always be thankful for the gift that he gave me—the Aristotelian principle of identity—a tool for daydreaming that I could always use, even during my later Zen Buddhist period in college, when I doubted the truth of it.

Color Guard

O ne of the rewards of high school athletics was receiving a letter. At Bonner the letters were embroidered green B's, with a symbol of your sport sewn into the center. The stitching that produced the letter was very much like looped carpet fabric. The letter was actually a little miniature rug in the shape of a B.

There were three sizes: varsity, the largest; junior varsity, about three-quarter size; and freshman, the smallest, about one-third the size of the varsity.

I only received one letter, and it wasn't exactly for a sport, it was for being on the drill team, Color Guard. The insignia in the middle of the B was a simple five-pointed star.

One day in the beginning of my second year, the entire sophomore class was called down to the auditorium to hear a spiel about the glories of being in the band by the band leader, Mr. Dougherty. We were surprised to find out that you didn't have to actually play an instrument to be in the band, you could begin taking lessons, free lessons, on borrowed instruments after school.

Mr. Dougherty's demonstration consisted of handing out instruments to random boys who were invited to hold them and, based on hints from the band leader, make noises by blowing through the mouthpieces in various ways. When it came round to the trumpet, I was one of the volunteers—a shill, actually, since I had been a bugler at Boy Scout camp, so I knew how to do the lips. Although it was an entertaining assembly, and some kids did sign up on the spot, it sounded like too much work to me.

Then, almost in passing, Mr. Dougherty mentioned the Color Guard. Onto the stage came two guys in uniform carrying rifles, and I began to reconsider. No instruments to learn, great uniforms to wear. When they started doing a drill with their rifles that included tossing them into the air, I was pretty much sold on the idea.

I had always liked uniforms, ever since I acquired my first one as a Cub Scout when I was seven or eight. The Bonner band uniforms, which the Color Guard shared, were composed of gray wool pants with a green and white stripe down the outside seam, and green wool coats, as well as a green officer's hat. I signed up that day and was scheduled for a uniform-fitting for after school on Thursday of that week. It was as simple as that, no real tryouts.

After the fitting on Thursday, there was a meeting for prospective members of the Color Guard, all of whom were accepted into the ranks, bringing the number of active members to four, plus the leader of the Color Guard, Bill Murphy. The Color Guard room was a small one just off the band room below the stage in the auditorium. The band room was designed like an amphitheater, built on levels so the entire band could see the director, who had a podium at the front from which he gave directions.

Murphy explained to us that we were going to get new rifles soon, but for now we would learn the drills on the old rifles, which were in pretty bad shape. We were told that uniforms would be provided but that we would have to buy our own black shoes and white cotton gloves. Since I always wore black shoes, anyway, I was relieved that I wouldn't have to invest any real money. My dad was on active duty at the time, and there wasn't a lot of extra cash lying around the house. I had tried out for the tennis team the year before but couldn't follow up on it because of the expense of the new sneakers that I would have to get if I continued. I figured white gloves wouldn't be too expensive.

That day we went out in our school clothes to practice the Manual of Arms and the marching. It was fairly easy for me because I knew a lot of the foot movements and positions from Boy Scouts. I knew the dance of Right Face and Left Face and the slightly complex positioning of About Face, so I was a little ahead of my peers at the start. Column Left and Right were new to me, however, as were the commands for the rifle positions. In Scouts we never needed such commands, since we never bore arms, even though Lord Baden-Powell had invented the Scouts for the purpose of training young Englishmen for the twentieth century's world wars. Playing Army when I was younger, we had marched and drilled a little bit, but we had always made it up as we went along. Now I was learning a new science, and having a great time at it too.

The highlight of that day, actually, was a particular series of moves called the Queen Anne's Salute, which began with the body at attention and the rifle, or "piece" as we learned to call it, on the right shoulder, and ended in a genuflection with the butt of the rifle on the ground, having wheeled it once through the air. I don't know who Queen Anne was, but she must have been pretty amazing to deserve such a sweet salute. Then again it may be that the salute existed before the queen.

I think, even then, I recognized the whole thing as a kind of manly dance, the members of the Color Guard being kinds of primo ballerinos, with the corps de ballet behind them, providing music for their more complicated steps. The idea of guarding the flag never occurred to me to be a frivolous thing, but rather noble and edifying. Besides, this was a sport that included no real physical contact or competition, but rather individual performance of prescribed motions. A truly cooperative sport.

The trip to the Army–Navy store to purchase the white gloves promised to be fun as well. Army–Navy stores have always been intriguing places for me. I had first visited one in third grade when I went to buy a bookbag for school. In first grade I got a plaid oilcloth one. Two years later, it felt too young for me; meanwhile, a certain kind of surplus bag had become all the rage. It was designed to hold a gas mask; in fact, Robin Bates had gotten a bag with a gas mask included. It was an interesting thing, olive oilcloth with two glassed eyeholes and a proboscis that held some kind of canister for oxygen or something. But it wasn't much use except to look at, and it pretty much blinded the wearer in our games of Army.

The important part was the bag it came in—and its long adjustable strap, the lengthening of which allowed the owner to wear it in several ways. Short, it could be slung over the shoulder; medium length, it could be worn as a backpack, with the middle of the strap across the back and the remainder of the strap on the shoulders, once the bag was flipped over the head; full length, it could be fixed so that the shoulder straps crossed in front of the chest (this was accomplished by twirling the thing a half-time in front) before they looped over the shoulders.

There were three brass buttonhole clasps through which fit curious little brass knob buttons that kept the thing closed. It had a U.S. on the flap. Sometimes we added messages of our own. When Batista was run out of Cuba when I was in the seventh grade, my strap read *Batista Fleas,* my version of the newspaper headlines of the day.

But on this day, I had no use for bags. I was there for gloves. As I entered the store I was hit by the delightful smell of army surplus mildew, and my eyes, growing accustomed to the light, roamed over the packs of various sizes hanging from the ceiling, shelves full of metal mess kits, collapsible trench shovels, tent spikes, and other paraphernalia I could have used if I were going camping—but no white gloves to be seen. I looked for a section with uniforms and saw some trench coats hanging in the back of the store, beyond the busy attendant's register. No one was available to help me, so I went back there by myself, pausing for a moment to see the medallions and patches showing rank and specialty.

I'd always been fascinated by this aspect of military gear, and had spent some time when I was younger memorizing the ranks listed on a colorful chart in the *World Book Encyclopedia.* Here there was no such chart to list all of the specialties and symbols of the regiments, and I tried to figure out what they might mean. Then on back to where the trench coats were hanging, in search of white gloves.

Besides the trench coats there were other pieces of Army, Navy, and Marine uniforms, and below these racks I found a plastic box filled with my quarry—white gloves. There were two boxes, actually; one held simple gloves for seventy-five cents, and the other held ones with a metal button. I tried the former on first. They were all right, but when I felt the richness of the second—thicker cotton, well-sewn seams—there was really no question, even though they were more than twice as expensive.

I tried several pairs on till I got ones that fit perfectly (my hands wouldn't grow that much anymore, so there was no need to buy one size larger, as was always my mother's philosophy when it came to school clothes) and walked up to the counter to pay for them.

"White gloves, eh?" said the old guy at the counter. "What are you gonna use these for? They're no good in the cold, you know, not thick enough."

"Don't need 'em for the cold, I'm on the drill team," I reported proudly, hoping the other two clerks would hear and be impressed. "Bonner's drill team," I continued, guessing at his next question.

"Oh, drill team, huh?" the guy drawled, ringing up the purchase on a manual cash register. "Need a rifle? We got some dummy rifles just came in, wanna see them?"

I winced at the belittlement implied at the word "dummy," though this was the correct name for a rifle that had been denuded of the hardware that made it lethal. But I was interested now in things artilleryesque, so I said, "Sure, where they at?"—speaking ungrammatically on purpose to fit into my blue-collar surroundings.

"In the back." Then to one of the other clerks, "Joe, show this kid the new rifles," motioning me to follow the other guy.

I picked up the bagged gloves and my change from the counter and followed. We went through what could have been a dressing-room door to another room, where I saw the guns in boxes laid out on a shelf. I walked over and picked one up. It was a little heavier than the ones back at school, and unlike them, it wasn't broken—the muzzle was intact, and the strap was obviously new.

I held it as militarily as I could, then opened the chamber in like manner, a move I had only learned two days before, partly showing off for the guy, partly impressing myself with my skill.

I blew out a little sawdust, then, with the air of a drill sergeant, closed the chamber and placed the piece on my shoulder. It felt great. I twirled it once and saw that the balance was the same as the ones at school, in fact the stock was probably standard, though the hardware on this one was chromed. The wood was painted white.

"Ours are unpainted, just shellacked," I said officiously.

"But how much is it?"

"Eight bucks each, ten for sixty," came the reply.

"Pretty good price," I responded. "Especially for ten," not knowing the actual value of the things. "I'll tell them at school."

I placed the rifle back in its wrapping and left the store, waving in response to the old guy's "Come again."

As soon as I was out of sight of the store, I took the gloves out and threw away the bag. Holding them in one hand, I slapped them into the other palm as I had seen Nazi officers do in movies as they questioned captured Americans. "You are surprised I understand your language, eh, Joe? I vent four years to your Harvard, and there I learned the decadent vays of your culture."

After a few of these moves I put them on and buttoned them, then tightened the fit by pushing them down into the spaces between my fingers. Once they were as tight as they could be, I began to take them off, finger by finger, imitating Fred Astaire's style as I did. Alternating between Nazi officer and debonair dancer, I walked home with my new treasure.

The next day I told Murphy about the rifles at the Army–Navy store, but he told me it was too late, ours had been ordered the week before, at an even cheaper price, and in fact should be in by the end of the week.

When they finally did come, it was clear why we had gotten such a good price. The stocks were unfinished—no paint, no shellac. So one day after school, instead of drilling we had a shellac party. We each did our own, with Murphy putting the final touches of black paint to trim the butt and the edge where stock met barrel. It took them several days to completely dry, and they stood on the rack like untouchable icons until the following Monday, when we finally got to use them in drill. Our uniforms came in that Tuesday, so we were ready to go. My pants were a little long, so I went to my Aunt Fran, who lived next door to us and had a sewing machine, and she fixed them fine.

The following Sunday would be my debut as a full member of the Color Guard at the football game with West Catholic. The night before I spit-shined my shoes eight or nine times in preparation, so I was more than ready to take the field. We met at the school and were bused out to the Villanova University stadium where we played our home games (Villanova being run by the same order of priests as Bonner). Jim Molloy, the other new kid on the team, and I sat together.

On the ride out, we played Twenty Questions. At one point Jim asked me if I was nervous.

"Not too much, I just hope I don't drop the rifle in the middle of a twirl," I said, surprised to be telling the truth when a bravado lie would have been more appropriate.

"Ever drop it before?" asked my friend, wisely.

"Not yet."

"Well, then?" he responded, leaving me to figure out the rest of the equation.

The energy in the stands at a Bonner football game was always amazing, but this would be the first time I would enter the stadium on the field, rather than the back stairs into the fan section, which entrance always muted the energy blast by placing one in the middle of it. Now, since I was official, I was entering from the field itself, and the sight and sound of the screaming throng was almost overwhelming. We didn't march in—we wouldn't be called upon to strut our stuff until halftime—but the energy was palpable, especially that day.

Bonner and West were arch-rivals, since the parishes from which they drew their respective students were contiguous; in fact, Bonner had taken over some of the parishes that had sent their boys to West since forever, so this competition was especially fierce. Long before such a game started, the respective cheerleading squads began whipping their fans into a frenzy, and the game was often followed by a fight right after.

I looked up into the stands and saw a few kids I recognized from class, who gestured back to me how sharp I looked. I pretended to take a shot at a few of them, until Murphy came over and told me to knock it off. I sat down, my rifle between my legs, and watched as the game began. With about three minutes to go in the first half, we received the signal to get ready to go on the field. We got up, Color Guard and band, and made our way to the end zone whence we would march onto the field for the halftime performance. Our job this time would be easy, a regular march on to the field, marking time in place as the band went through its paces, then a few moves as the colors were presented, including my favorite, the Queen Anne, a few twirls in place, back to attention, and then the march off. We had practiced the moves for several days, although only once with the full band on the field at Bonner. My only real concern had to do with the new gloves. We had not practiced at all with them. And they were somewhat slippery, to tell the truth.

Mr. Dougherty looked great. His uniform was all white, though with the same striping and shoulder cords that we had. Next to him stood the drum major, who had the best outfit of anyone, a great high hat and a marvelous two-toned cape— white wool on the outside, green satin on the inside. The Bonner green was a serious green—not kelly green, not aquamarine, but deep ocean green. Real green.

A gunshot rang out, marking the end of the half, and as the teams headed for the locker rooms, we stood at attention, watching the drum major. Murphy shouted "Right Shoulder Arms!," meant just for us. We obeyed.

Our goal was to cross to the far twenty-yard line, then turn and stand "at ease" (our feet apart, rifle butt at right toe, muzzle held out and away from the body) until the band had finished its maneuvers. But on the way, Murphy got it into his head to show off a little bit.

Out of nowhere, it seemed, he shouted out, "Trail Arms!" This meant that the piece should come off our right shoulders to Port Arms, then our right hand should grab the stock near the muzzle and hold it out at an angle like in At Ease, but without the butt touching the ground—as we marched all the while.

It was not a difficult order to follow, at least for a few seconds, the normal time we would have to hold the piece at this position. But Murphy must have gotten distracted, because we ended up holding this position for a longer period than usual. And I began to feel the rifle slip, a result of a combination of slippery gloves and wrist fatigue.

As I marched, I considered my options: let it drop and march on unarmed; stop and pick it up, risking collision with the clarinets in the front row of the band; or invent a new move which would get it back in my hands higher up where it was secure. None of these options seemed desirable.

I tried to signal Murphy about my problem, but the band was too loud. Finally I could wait no longer. What I did amounted to pretending that Murphy had given the order to shoulder my arms—that is, I let the butt hit the ground and flipped it forward, catching it below the trigger with my left hand, and twirled it up to my right shoulder, regrasping the butt with my right hand. Molloy apparently thought he had missed Murphy's command, and on the next left foot, he did the same thing. On the other side of the colors Kelly saw the flash of

Molloy's piece, and on the next left step shouldered his piece with the same maneuver, leaving our fourth man, Lang, no choice but to do the same on the next left step.

Just then we were passing the "reviewing stand," the section where the principal sat. Murphy screamed, a little louder than necessary, "Eyes Left!," and when my eyes went left, I could see Murphy's face. Steam was rising from the ears as they reddened in anger. I thought I could see him say silently through gritted teeth, "You're going to get it, Stivender," but I couldn't be sure.

When we reached the twenty-yard line, we turned and stood at ease as the band did its thing. I spent the time wondering what I would do with the white gloves now that I was going to be thrown off the team. Then we marched back, and the crowd roared its appreciation.

We returned to the stands and sat down. I waited for Murphy to yell at me, but he chose the silent treatment instead. I knew I would get it when we got back to the school. The other three in the guard were talking among themselves, trying to figure out what had happened. Everybody was afraid of approaching Murphy. We won the game, and the subsequent fight was a brief one.

As we were reboarding the buses, Mr. Dougherty came over to Murphy and drew him aside. I was surprised to see he was smiling. Murphy was nodding, and then he began to smile as well. Not a word was spoken on the way back. Nothing was said the next Monday at practice, but when Murphy started teaching us the proper way to do the Consecutive Shoulder Arms command, as he called my invention (though without giving me credit), I began to relax, and even congratulate myself. I had expanded my team's repertoire because of my slippery new gloves. And I wasn't thrown off the team.

Murphy's anger never totally subsided, however, taking various forms of subtle mistreatment—hostile inspections, exclusion from interesting assignments—and Color Guard became more of a burden than a joy. I got my letter at the end of the year, but it wasn't the varsity one I thought I deserved. I didn't return the following year.

About a year ago, going through some stuff in my mother's basement, I found a paper bag that held old Boy Scout badges and those white gloves, now brown with age but with the buttons still intact. I slipped them on, stood up, and tried a Queen Anne's Salute with a baseball bat. It wasn't the same. I guess you have to have music playing behind you. And the colors, of course, and Molloy and Kelly and Lang—and Murphy.

The Great Debate

*B*y the time I got to senior year at Bonner, my role in Section 4S3 was fairly well established. My peers knew me for my excellent timing of wisecracks and my general fund of knowledge. I used to read the Epprights' encyclopedia for pleasure, a volume at a time.

The Epprights were our cousins, the result of my Aunt Fran marrying a Marine named Ed, who came from southwest Philadelphia.

Southwest Philadelphia was also where our neighbors the Forbeses had moved from. Mr. Forbes and Uncle Ed knew each other from the old neighborhood, I think; at any rate, they spoke with the same accent. An accurate philologist could probably graph the accents of the Delaware Valley block by block. They are quite distinctive, and you can always tell someone from Philadelphia by their nasal *a*'s and clipped *o*'s. I lost my own accent in college trying to do Shakespeare, and I sometimes regret the loss; I could use it in my current profession as a monologist. It returns only at Thanksgiving and Christmas, when I'm around my family, and on Mummers' Day, when I'm in the parade with real Philadelphians.

Having cousins next door was a blessing. They must have had more money than us to be able to get the encyclopedia, but having them there was just as good as having our own, especially with their liberal loan policy. Our doors were always open in those days, and I would just go in and take a volume, shouting out to my Aunt Fran, "I'm taking Volume Eight!"

"OK! Have a good time!" would come the reply, and I'd go home, get comfortable, and read.

I was better read than most of my peers. Section 4S3 was about fifth of seventeen classes, still on the "scientific" track, thus the *S*. The two highest tracks were honors, 4H1 and 4H2. There were two *S* tracks below us in academic standings. I think if I had been more serious, I would have been in one of these *H*'s. But when I should have been doing my real homework, I'd be reading the encyclopedia. I was a sponge, but not very disciplined.

In English, my classmates dubbed me the "Literary Dictator of 4S3"—the title reserved for Samuel Johnson in his eighteenth-century London coffeehouse set—because of the way I often volleyed with our teacher, Mr. Simmons, questioning him on his use of vocabulary and sometimes his assignments. He was fairly good-humored about it. As an ectomorphic layman, he understood my mode on some level.

With Father McGilligan, it was different. He was a mesomorphic priest—one of the Augies, as we called them—and he did not enjoy my humor. He may have been tipped off by the other Augustinians that had me the year before, perhaps my Latin III teacher, who was the least tolerant of any of my instructors. Usually there was a getting-to-know-each-other period at the beginning of a school year where the teacher and the class clown would feel each other out in a kind of intellectual sparring, finding what the limits were with a detention or two and then settling into a putting-up-with-each-other relationship that would last the year. But McGilligan seemed to be waiting for my first move from the first day.

He was the only teacher to give me a nickname almost immediately: "Stivey." He would use it with a vocal attitude attached. I'll admit that because of the class he was teaching, he was at a real disadvantage, a little more vulnerable to me and my guild of debating clowns. The name of the class was Apologetics. Although it sounds like it might have to do with manners and etiquette—i.e., how to apologize correctly for a faux pas—it was in reality just the opposite. Apologetics was the scholastic science of proving the truths of the faith through (sometimes contentious) debate.

Religion class in high school always had a measure of natural debate to it. It was the great joy and awful responsibility of the class clown to bring up issues and points of argument concerning aspects of the faith and practice of Roman Catholicism in this most required of classes. One of the favorite topics was the fairness of Limbo and Hell—why certain people could not get into Heaven through no fault of their own—second only to the paradox of free will and predestination.

There was somewhere in the long Catholic tradition an answer for every question that could possibly be raised, but not every priest knew every one of these answers. We would badger the poor guy until he fell back to the inevitable position: "It's a mystery, we won't know until we get to Heaven." Although this seemed to end any argument in stalemate, it was in fact a clear victory for the questioner and an implicit surrender by the teacher.

This intellectual conflict happened in all Religion classes, no matter what the supposed curriculum for the year. But the teacher of the senior course was in a special kind of bind: presenting arguments to show the truth of the Faith was the purpose of the course. To lose an argument in this setting would be ignoble. To fight to the draw of "mystery" would clearly be a loss, an acceptance of the fact that the arguments presented could not do the job required.

We must have gotten off on a very bad footing, McGilligan and I, because he was using his pet nickname in the snide tone of voice early on. He was also the only priest to use ad hominem arguments against me, commenting on my appearance or dress. Ad hominem—literally, "at the man"—is the rhetorical device whereby the debater attacks the argument by attacking the arguer. It's low on the list of effective debate strategies, and everyone in the senior class knew it.

One Friday afternoon found us in heated conversation about some topic or other, with McGilligan getting madder and madder as we went on. Finally, he threw up his hands and ended the debate. Then, in a voice that clearly conveyed punishment, he said:

"All right, Stivey, we'll give you a chance to have the floor next week, all to yourself and one of the other students. We're going to have a debate, boys, one on each side, and Stivey, you will take the con side, the against side. The topic of the debate will be The Existence of God."

I felt the sharpness of his weapon here very clearly. It was a setup to make me look foolish, so that I would calm down and hold my tongue for the rest of the year. It was a no-win situation for me. How could anyone prevail in such a contest? Everyone knew that God existed, how could anyone doubt it? I certainly never did. I prayed to God every day, went to Communion several times a week—Bonner had Communion services right before lunch every day in the chapel, they were optional but my friends and I normally attended—and went to Confession on the weekends. McGilligan was obviously setting me up for failure.

The priest continued, "Your opponent will be John Brum-field." Brumfield was a quiet kid from Pius X Parish. Everyone knew he was real smart, plus there was something numinous about him, he had a scar that went all the way across his cheek, marking him as someone blessed in a special way. We never asked him where the scar came from, but we knew he had escaped something with his life.

I was pretty much doomed. I would try my best in this impossible task, but surely Brumfield would win the debate in one day. I would be shamed and have to spend the rest of the year quiet in my seat, under the thumb of the black robe. I had the weekend to plan my strategy.

After classes I went to the Bonner library and asked Father Menihan if he had any books by atheists that disproved the existence of God. He didn't laugh at me outright—perhaps he knew what McGilligan was up to—but he said no, there were no such books in *his* library, maybe I would have better luck at the public library. I might want to look, however, in the *Catholic Encyclopedia* to see what it had to say about the existence of God.

The *Catholic Encyclopedia!* What a great idea, I thought. I was familiar enough with the joys of the *World Book* at the Epprights', but a whole encyclopedia with just Catholic stuff would be wonderful. He turned to the reserve shelf and picked up a green volume and handed it to me.

"Just look up 'God: existence of,'" he said, smiling benignly.

The volume was much heavier than the volumes of the *World Book* at the Epprights', and there were no color pictures. The language, too, was quite a bit denser, which turned out to be to my advantage, because if I had understood the sentences I would surely have despaired.

The article was composed of arguments to prove God's existence, and there were many of them. From the chapter headings I learned at least the names of some of the issues: *Proof from Order, Proof from Scripture, Unmoved Mover, The Arguments Against the Nominalists, The Ontological Argument.* I read a few lines under this last heading and came across a marvelous concept—"that than which there is no greater."

It was the phrasing "that than which" that fascinated me. To carry this kind of a concept in my mind was new to me. "Than which." I said it over and over, trying to let it make some sense. I knew there was something there, not so much for my case against the existence of God, but for my future thoughts on this and other subjects. I closed the volume, and returned it to the desk, where Father received it smiling.

"Find anything?"

"Oh, yes, I found something than which much is more helpful," I said, and left the room, proud of my new phrase, wondering if I had said a meaningful sentence. The look on the priest's face gave me no feedback. And so down to the public library in Upper Darby.

My mind was feeling stretched a bit, and I was beginning to enjoy it. McGilligan had unknowingly raised me to a higher level of discourse with his challenge, and though I would surely lose, I resolved to go down arguing. The task was seeming less impossible by the hour.

The librarian in the public library was surprised by my request for information on arguments against the existence of God, and she told me to look in the card catalog under *atheism.* I did so. My search yielded two names, Jean-Paul Sartre and Friedrich Nietzsche. I went to the books that were listed and looked through them, dismayed by the obscurity of the language. Even if I understood it, it would be difficult sharing the knowledge with my peers and McGilligan.

But then a heading in the Nietzsche book caught my eye: *The Death of God.* Hmmmm. Maybe God used to exist but didn't any longer. I rejected the possibility that this was true, but it started my mind thinking along the lines of change, and deep inside a trace of an argument began to emerge, subtly and quietly. It would germinate over the weekend, and if the debate went longer than a day's class period, it would blossom into a strategy. I thanked the librarian and left for home.

It was an interesting weekend. On Saturday I took a walk down to Darby Creek in the afternoon to do some thinking. I knew Darby Creek would afford me some space and time for rumination. The day was beautiful, Indian summer, but I was offended by its beauty. Surely one of the arguments that Brumfield would present was the argument about Creation—how could it be so beautiful without a divine mind ordering it so?

As I sat on a rock overhanging the water, a couple of boys, a few years younger than I, appeared fifty yards downstream, carrying a burlap bag between them. Something was squirming in the bag. I suspected it was a cat. I was right. They shook the bag, and out it dropped. Its feet were tied. It lay on the pebbly beach writhing and wailing as the kids kicked it around. Then one of them picked up a large stone at the water's surface, lifted it above his head and brought it down hard on the cat's head. After that the cat was still. The bigger of the two then pushed it with his foot into the stream and it half floated, half dragged downstream. The kids watched it go, threw a couple of stones at it, then walked up the bank and disappeared.

My heart was racing. Although I knew there was nothing I could have done—a task as far along in its execution as this one would not have been affected by a few shouts across the creek—I felt sort of guilty, not for what I had done or not done, but for what members of my species had done to another species. Then came into my mind all kinds of justifications: the cat was sick, the cat had mauled a little kid, the cat was part of the overpopulation problem.

And then my disgust was tempered with the realization that what I had just seen was applicable to my case. Man's cruelty to animals might be a proof that God does not exist, and if cruelty to animals was an argument, how about cruelty to other humans? How about war? If God existed he wouldn't let war happen.

This didn't feel like a really strong argument, since war and the Catholic religion were pretty tied up with one another. In third grade, I had won an essay contest for a piece about Fighting Father Duffy, a chaplain in the First World War, so I knew that God being on our side in war was an important thing. I would be going against a lot of tradition if I were to use this argument. President Kennedy, the year before, had made the Russians back down in Cuba, and surely in a war against the Communists, God would be on our side, if there was a God. We had learned that the Communists didn't believe in God. Perhaps our victories in Cuba and Korea were proof of the validity of Christianity against the atheistic Communists.

But maybe by cutting around the idea of "sides" I could gain a few points. I would have to make sure to show that it was the existence of evil that proved God didn't exist, because if he did, he wouldn't let evil occur, that is if he *were* all-powerful, which he had to be if he were God—"that than which there is no greater."

That than which there is no greater. The phrase kept ringing in my mind. I tried to make up other sentences with this structure. Bonner's football team was that than which there is no greater. Kennedy was the president than which there was no Catholicer. America was the country than which there was no democraticer. The problem with this line of thinking was that one had to make up words that didn't really exist. Perhaps that would help me.

The debate was going to be judged by the kids in the class, not by McGilligan himself, so that was one good thing, although I wasn't sure how many of my classmates would be clear that a vote for my side didn't necessarily mean that they were atheists themselves.

I tried to bring to mind the arguments that Brumfield would present. Order, beauty—my cruelty-and-war argument could handle these. And then there was "Everybody throughout history has believed in some kind of God." Hmmmm. Easy one—if everybody throughout history jumped off a cliff ...

I went home that afternoon a little encouraged, at least I was ready for some of what would be brought up. At three-thirty I went to church to go to Confession. All the thinking about God had made me a little nervous about my standing with Him, and I wanted to clear it up. When it was my turn, I entered the booth and knelt down, listening to the inaudible mumble on the other side of the little door that hid the priest until he was finished with the sinner in the other booth. The door slid back, and through the screen I was relieved to see the face of the Norbertine priest who was assigned to the parish. He taught at one of the other high schools and gave great sermons, at least my mother thought so. Best of all, he wouldn't recognize my voice.

"Bless me, Father, for I have sinned. It has been one week since my last confession ..." My confessions were pretty much the same since grade school—disobedience, lying—though lately I had discovered the dangerous joy of impure thoughts. After I had cataloged my usual, I paused, and the priest said:

"Is there anything else?"

"Well ... yes, there is." I paused and gulped and continued. "Is it a sin to not believe in God?"

"Well, my son, that depends on whether your disbelief is a result of culpable or inculpable ignorance. If you've never heard of God—say, you're on an island in the South Pacific not visited by missionaries—it is no sin, but if you have heard about God, you surely would believe in Him, else where would all our blessings come from but God, the unmoved mover? Surely *you* don't disbelieve in God, else why would you be here today?"

"Yes, Father, but I have to be in a debate to prove the nonexistence of God. And I want to win, but I don't want to sin. Winning without sinning, is it possible to do that?"

He chuckled, perhaps at the unintentional rhyme of it. "Oh, my son, taking part in a school activity is never a sin. Do you know what 'mental reservation' is?"

In fact I did. "Isn't that when a prisoner of the Communist Chinese betrays his God and country in words, but in his heart stays faithful under torture?" There had been a lot of talk about the GI's that had been captured in Korea and cracked under the pressure of cruel interrogation.

"Yes, that's one example. As long as you keep the mental reservation that God exists in your heart, you won't be in danger of sin."

"But what if I win?"

"No need to worry about that. Is your teacher a priest?"

"Yes." *But he's a jerk*, I mentally reserved.

"Then I'm sure he won't let you win, and you have nothing to worry about."

Great.

"Now for your penance, say three Our Fathers and three Hail Marys and pray for God's forgiveness, and watch those impure thoughts."

That's the problem, Padre, I thought. *I do watch them.*

I tried not to watch them too closely that night at the Holy Cross teen dance, and the chaperons only tapped me on the shoulder once, when I was dancing too slow with Diane Kunstler. She was from Drexel Hill, and one of the loveliest girls in Prendergast, the girls' school. I asked her if I could see her home. She said yes, even though we had to take a bus and walk. The walk gave us a chance to talk.

"Do you believe in God, Diane?"

"Of course, silly rabbit, everyone believes in God. How could a person not believe in God? Where else would this come from"—moving her hands down her waist to show off her sweet slim body—"if not from God?" she asked. Laughing, inviting.

I put my hand on her waist and she caught it, keeping it from moving any higher, "Oh, no you don't."

I was tempted to tell her how her sweetness could be the focus of impure thoughts in me, thus implying an argument against the existence of God. But the night was not one for such conversation, so I stole a chaste kiss, and she ran ahead.

"Tell me you don't believe in God," she teased, turning in her tracks, "when at least one part of His creation proves his existence so clearly."

I took a few quick steps to grab her, grabbed air instead, and the race was on, all the way back to her house, me letting her win. Really. A kiss at the door and I was on my way back home.

Was Diane Kunstler's existence an argument for or against the existence of God? Deep in my groin a million sperm cried, "For! For!" I wasn't so sure.

Throughout my classes on Monday I was distracted by my approaching task. Finally, it was time for Religion. McGilligan had borrowed a second lectern from somewhere and set up the room for the debate, his lectern serving the *pro* side, the borrowed one for the *against* side.

"Well then, boys, we are ready to start the great debate." McGilligan went to the board with a piece of chalk, speaking as he wrote:

RESOLVED: GOD EXISTS.

"The debate will continue until all arguments and counterarguments are heard. Then there will be a vote, and the majority of the votes will decide who won. Mr Brumfield, you may begin with the presentation of your first statement."

Brumfield must have gotten a new jacket for this day, and a haircut too—he did look natty. He had a bunch of notes written on loose-leaf paper. He read directly from them, looking at the class occasionally.

"I thank God that I have a chance to defend His existence against my adversary in this debate. Whom else should I thank? It is God who gave *me* existence. Why should I doubt his, therefore? It is God who gave us this wonderful day, as he gave us all of Creation in six. It is God who gave us this land of America, and the one nation under Him, as we recite every day. Why should I doubt the Founding Fathers, who gave us this pledge? I ask your prayers, my brothers, that I may prove unrevocably His existence, as though it needed to be proven at all, and I beg you to pray for my poor misled brother, Ed Stivender, that his arguments lead not one of us to doubt either the existence of God or the impossibilities of the arguments he will present to us."

As he returned to his seat, I mouthed a question: *Unrevocably?* He shrugged good-naturedly.

I took the podium and lay down my notes on the surface. And paused. Longer than I thought I could, looking around the room for effect. I knew I had allies in that room (the other class clowns were on my side, at least), but I had to defuse the feeling that I was on the edge of blasphemy. If I could only hold my own for a class period, I might have a chance to win.

"Father McGilligan, Mr. Brumfield, brother Catholics, patron saints"—this looking up—"souls in Purgatory, Blessed Mother, Holy Trinity."

I paused, proud of my opening, classical as it was, putting myself in the court of the Communion of Saints and acknowledging myself as a Catholic at the outset. Had the tone in the room been different, I would have gotten a laugh, but I didn't want one, not yet, so I didn't address the ghosts that might be standing invisibly around, nor the PA system that might have been turned on by the disciplinarian who might be listening to this. The art of timing is a classical art, and I knew intuitively I was riding a dangerous line.

"I, too, pray to God, for help in this debate, that He will make my opponent think clearly and speak clearly in this discussion, that he may help you listen clearly and receive what I have to say in the good faith it was intended. For if God does exist, my proof of His nonexistence will not matter to Him one jot, one tittle"—I figured using biblical language could only help me—"and if He does not exist, then none of any of this matters to anyone except perhaps to each one of us individually, and to me most of all."

I knew what I was saying did not make any real sense, but I hoped that my style would carry me, as it seemed to be doing.

"Some of you may be threatened by the idea that God doesn't exist, because if he does not, then our faith as Catholics is in vain, but I say, no, if God does not exist, our faith is made nobler, our decision to continue as Catholics approaches the heroic. For what can be nobler in the face of the darkness that surrounds us than for us to believe in something that is impossible. Only in doing something that is impossible does man achieve his final goal; assenting to being when nothingness surrounds him is what makes a man a man."

McGilligan was frowning. I was on a roll. I was happy that I was able to use at least the title of the Sartre book too dense for me to read.

"But before I go on, I want to make sure from Father that voting for my side at the end of the debate is in no way a sin, for I would be loath"—just the week before I had learned this word in vocabulary in Simmons' class—"to lead any of my brother Catholics into scandal." Then looking at McGilligan directly: "Father, can you assure us that this debate is not an occasion of sin, even if the con side were to win?"

McGilligan, frowning. "No, Mr. Stivender, voting for your side will not be a sin."

"Thank you, Father, and so, my fellow Catholics, I beg you to listen well and then to use your own free will, the greatest gift we have." And then I sat down.

McGilligan called Brumfield to the lectern again. He began by reading Joyce Kilmer's poem, "Trees," slowly and forcefully—with extra emphasis on the punchline, "But only *God* can make a tree"—and expounding on the argument from Creation. With all the beauty and order in the world, there must be an orderer, a beautifier. It was actually a well-done job, reading the poem eased the tension and raised the level of discourse.

As he was finishing up, I scrambled in my memory for a poem to throw back; luckily, Robert Frost's "Fire and Ice" was available. I took my place at the lectern and began to recite, spitting out the last lines with as much venom as I could muster: "I think I know enough of hate / To say, that for destruction ice / Is also great / And would suffice."

"Ice, gentlemen, ice, the great destroyer," I continued. "Look out the window there, see the trees? Sure, they are beautiful now, but soon it will be winter and there will be ice storms, and the ice will bring trees down to their death. Death, gentlemen, is death beautiful? No. What about maggots in a garbage pail, are they beautiful? What about polio? Is that beautiful?" We still had memories of kids who had died of it in the '50s.

"What about earthquakes, fires, landslides, tidal waves, uh, uh"—I was reaching here, trying to figure out some more natural disasters—"famines, floods, are they beautiful? If God exists, why does he let these things happen?"

I paused here, a long time. "Why? Why? There are two possibilities. Either he wants them to happen, in which case you can't really say he is good, and what can you do with a non-good God? It's a contradiction in terms. God is supposed to be that than which there is no greater, but anyone who sees the horror is then greater than God."

I knew this one was weak, but I kept going.

"The other possibility is that God can't stop these disasters, in which case he is not much of a God. Either way, there is no real God in the picture. A tree is poor proof for the existence of God if a wildfire that brings the tree down cannot be stopped by the tree's creator."

I was almost frothing at the mouth, wondering where these ideas were coming from, proud of my speed. Some of my classmates were sitting there wide-eyed. McGilligan was frowning. I couldn't see Brumfield's eyes, he was writing on his pad. I sat down. Silence.

Brumfield approached the lectern. He was in trouble now.

"Mr. Stivender has told us nothing new. We all know that there are tragedies in the world. But God knows why he allows them, it is not meant for us to know." He was on the verge of calling it a mystery, but to his credit, he did not use this tactic. It would have won him high marks from McGilligan but would have lost the day for him in the eyes of our classmates, who knew the line all too well, so he quickly moved on to his next argument.

He took out of his pocket two pool balls, a white one and a black one, and announced, "The argument from motion." He placed the black one on the ledge of the blackboard, about in the middle, then took the white one and rolled it toward the black one from a few feet away. They clicked, and the black one moved a few inches.

"I'll do it again. This time watch the eight ball and tell me how it comes to move."

He repeated the exercise then took the podium, leaving the balls on the ledge.

"The black ball moved because there was a cause of its movement, the white ball. And the white ball moved because of my hand. Nothing moves by itself. And everything moves, therefore, everything that moves must have a mover, and if you think back to the first movement, there must be an unmoved mover. That is God. He is the one responsible for every motion in the universe, and since he is God, he has no one moving behind him, or else he would not be perfect as God must be."

He sat down, proud of himself. It was a good argument, and I wondered if McGilligan had coached him.

I approached the balls on the ledge, not sure what I was going to do but knowing that their visual impact was more important than any argument I might give at this point. I picked up one of the balls, looked up to Heaven, and said, "Dear God, if you don't exist, please let this ball fall to the ground, and if you do exist, let it stay in the air."

I dropped it and it fell. The class laughed nervously. On some level I had scored a point. I did not pick it up.

"What did I just prove? That gravity is stronger than God? Perhaps. That my prayers do not move God? Perhaps. Perhaps they are not strong enough to move God to do something that I ask for, perhaps I am not pure enough." I hoped this wasn't true. "But if God is the unmoved mover, then why does anyone pray? If we didn't feel that our prayers could move God to do something on our behalf, we wouldn't pray. And if we can't move Him, then all our prayers are in vain. How many of you pray?"

Every hand went up.

"How many have had their prayers answered?"

A few hands came down.

"Most of you have therefore moved God through your prayers, therefore the existence of prayer proves that God is not the unmoved mover. Indeed, we can move Him"—an image of a moving van with several Bonner boys shoving a statue of God into it entered my mind, but I didn't laugh—"move Him to assist us, move Him to heed our prayers, move Him to help us with our schoolwork. Therefore, either praying is stupid or God can be moved. I rest my case."

A couple of kids applauded as I came to my conclusion, more from the drama of the moment than from the argument itself. I sensed that I was breaking some rule of grammar in this argument. When I thought about it later, I realized I used two different definitions for *move,* but I still made my point. Bloody business, this debate stuff.

Brumfield started for the front of the room, not excitedly, but McGilligan rose also and motioned for him to sit down.

"Well, boys, you've done well for today. Now I had expected to have the debate over in one period, but I suspect Mr. Brumfield and Stivey have more to say, so we'll let it go one more day. We only have a few minutes left, so you can use the rest of the period as a study."

I was overjoyed. I had lasted longer than McGilligan thought I could. Years later I remembered this moment as I watched the end of *Rocky*. I had gone the fifteen rounds and was still in the game. For it was a game, was it not?

When the bell rang, I went over to Brumfield and shook his hand. He smiled back, but he looked tired as he went to retrieve the pool balls from the front of the room. At some point, I think, Brumfield had decided to give me slack, to not punch holes in my weak arguments, to present his views simply, without bombast. I think it ultimately came down to a kind of lay solidarity. Brumfield knew that McGilligan was after me and that to some degree he was an involuntary accomplice.

I wanted to check the *G* volume of the *Catholic Encyclopedia* to look up the ontological argument. I had a feeling Brumfield would be using it, and I wanted to have a sense of it so I could respond when the time came. After school I went back to the library to look it up. The construction "that than which" intrigued me and haunted me at the same time.

The priest smiled as I asked for the volume, and I wondered how much these guys discussed the students with each other after school. I knew they talked over discipline cases—I had seen a kind of subtle persecution of certain kids who acted up in one class by teachers in other classes, as though there was an underground network of conversation. I didn't think of myself as a real discipline problem, I always pulled out of a behavior nose-dive before I crashed against the ground of rules dear to the teacher's heart, but I didn't know how this debate was echoing in the halls of the Augustinian residence, nor what effect it might have on my other classes.

I turned to the section and began to read slowly. The argument ran something like this: God is that than which nothing is greater; existence is greater than nonexistence; therefore God, by definition, exists. It was clear to me that the argument was too dependent on words. I sensed some kind of impropriety here, as though the philosophers who invented this argument, St. Ambrose being the most famous, were using words to conjure God. But I couldn't simply say that I knew that the secret lay in the "that than which" without knowing how to put it together.

I skimmed the rest of the article, picking up catch phrases so I would be familiar with some of the words that would come my way. Under a heading about Plato, I found a concept that surprised me—simplicity. Part of God's perfection came from the fact that he was "unmixed," simple, he could not be broken down into smaller pieces, nor could he decay or dissolve—unlike creatures, like ourselves.

My folk-singing friend Billy Stevenson used to sing the song, "Simple Gifts": "'Tis a gift to be simple ..." I wondered what the connection was, I knew it was there somewhere.

The library closed at four, and I started to hitchhike home. Hitchhiking gives you a lot of time to think, and I went over the possibilities of "that than which" in my mind. It was raining, but I had a good poncho and my shoes were almost waterproof.

"That than which nothing is perfecter." But existence would be part of perfection. "That than which nothing is more unmovable." But that would go against the movability argument I had presented that day. "That than which nothing is simpler" crossed my mind, and a roil in my stomach warned me I was on to something. The trick lay in the second premise: is existence connected to simplicity like it is to perfection and greatness?

The summer before, a friend of mine with whom I took the trolley, had become very depressed. One of the kids at school was picking on him because of his size. He had been one of the biggest kids in the class since our elementary years—always assigned the last place in the May Procession line, figured by size—but he was very gentlemanly, and this did not fit his size, and so one of the other kids had decided to pick on him, the way that Frankie Carr had picked on me freshman year.

But this persecution had been going on a long time, and one day my friend said he had decided to kill himself, because it was simpler than going on like that. I had tried to talk him out of it, and in fact he did not commit suicide, but it was not because I had been able to convince him that living life, with all its attendant hassles, would be simpler.

There it was. All right, it was another wordplay, of course, but at least it was a way out of an argument that seemed to be based on wordplay in the first place.

Plato says that simplicity is an aspect of God. God is that than which there is nothing more simple. Nonexistence is simpler than existence, therefore God does not exist. My stomach calmed down. I had a defensive weapon. It seemed to me that this debate thing was a little like the Communist–American arms race. I was stockpiling arguments to play against attack.

The next day, when I saw my friend on the trolley, I asked him how it was with his torturer.

"Actually it's going quite well. I decided the best weapon was to challenge him to a game of Indian leg wrestling during gym. But he passed up the challenge. He hasn't bothered me since last week."

"Glad to hear it."

At lunch, Brumfield was behind me in the tray line as we got our orange drink and layer cake. It was still rainy, and I was mad we wouldn't get a chance to go outside for fresh air after lunch. There was a little tension in the air, which he broke with one little comment. He gestured to the weather out the window and said.

"I wonder what farmer's prayers have moved God to tears."

As I looked him in the eyes, I got the feeling that he had figured through the loophole in my argument of the day before. I wondered if he would show it to the class today.

The classes that day moved quickly, and we soon found ourselves in McGilligan's class, the lecterns up front. The debate started late, however, because McGilligan wanted to lecture us on the immorality of a movie he had seen the night before and warn us against seeing it ourselves. Perhaps his real agenda was to remind us whose classroom it was.

Brumfield was in rare form when we finally did get started, up at the board with chalk trying to make the ontological argument make sense to a pack of seniors who weren't really interested but happy that the lecturer was one of their own.

There was little time on the clock when my turn came, but I wouldn't need much time. In fact, lack of time would keep Brumfield from seeing the flaw in my argument.

I walked to the front of the room. "In the *Catholic Encyclopedia* it says that Plato said that God is simple. If I were to take Mr. Brumfield's argument and apply this virtue of simplicity, I could show you that God is that than which nothing is simpler. Nonexistence is simpler than existence"—I shot a look at my friend from the trolley, who looked newly awakened from a daydream and smiled at me—"therefore God does not exist!" I hissed bombastically at the close of the sentence.

I expected a round of applause or some sign of recognition from my classmates, but the air in the room had become complex. Everyone was looking at McGilligan, and McGilligan was looking at me with anger in his eyes. Things were not going as he had planned. Then the bell rang, releasing all of us from our bonds of uncertainty. Day Two, and the debate was still going on.

The next day Brumfield reviewed the arguments I had presented in a lengthy recitation, trying to show how I had bent some words to get my way. I countered by attacking the ontological argument itself as mere wordplay.

When it was Brumfield's turn again, he rolled out a long poster with a time line showing the history of the world's religions, with colors and arrows noting all of the great religious reformations and movements worldwide. He spent a lot of time reciting the beliefs of each religion, and finally ended by saying that the greatest proof for the existence of God was the fact that mankind had always believed in Him, and why not, He had created him, given him the earth to rule over, starting the whole ball rolling. He ended by saying, "Ten billion believers can't be wrong."

It was extremely well done. But now it was my turn.

"Father McGilligan, brother Catholics, souls in Purgatory, St. Ambrose, Plato, and all the Communion of Saints"—I was deliberately slowing the pace of the discussion and formalizing it as I had done on the first day—"my noble opponent in this debate has presented a final argument. It is an argument for belief from belief. He wants you to believe that since mankind has always believed in God, therefore God exists. If all mankind jumped over a cliff, would you do it as well?"

I looked at my friend from the trolley, whose face was in the position of someone figuring something out. Then he looked at me and smiled and nodded. Some subliminal part of my brain was trying to work out his insight. Of course, if everyone went over the cliff, there wouldn't be much point in living, alone as one would be. No persecutors, of course, but no one to go to plays with ... Of course not.

Here I went to the board, drew a single horizontal line, and continued. "And after all, the time line of an individual is similar to the time line of culture, of the history of mankind.

When you're a kid, you believe your parents are God. But then you realize they are not"—all along, making dots and lines in and around to mark where a person might believe such things, then I zeroed in on about age eight—"and when you are little, you believe that Santa Claus exists. But now you know he does not." I paused, and asked, "Don't you?" Most nodded.

"Of course not, and it is the same way with God. When mankind was young, mankind believed in God, like we believed in Santa Claus. But now we are older, and as St. Paul says, now that we are older, we put away childish things."

I shot a look at McGilligan. He was frowning, his face was red.

"God is a crutch that we no longer need. Only babies and fairy boys need to believe in Santa Claus, only wusses need to believe in God. Even if He did exist, He wouldn't want us to remain children all our lives, now would He?"

I sat down to total silence. It occurred to me that some of my classmates had begun to worry about the fate of my immortal soul. If I really believed what I was saying, I was an atheist, and on my way to Hell. I didn't care about that as much as I cared about winning the debate. Now was the time for the vote, I felt, to see who won.

McGilligan went to his desk, and said, "The rest of the period is a study."

The next day the lecterns were gone, the debate was discontinued, we never had a vote. I had obviously won.

And now I was an object of discussion, myself. People were amazed to have an atheist in their midst, and kids would ask me with wonder in their eyes whether I really disbelieved in the existence of God. Usually I would maintain the role, it fit my place as Literary Dictator of 4S3, after all.

But one day, a few weeks later, my noble opponent asked me about it.

"So Stivey, how about it? Do you really not believe in God?"

"John, I have a confession to make," I said. "I still believe in Santa Claus."

He laughed.

"But he never gave me a present like the slack you cut me during that debate," I said. "Thanks."

"That than which no one is more welcome," he replied.

At the Cross

*F*ather Meyer, the pastor of Holy Cross Parish, had been a
chaplain in the United States Army in Europe during
World War II. Which meant he knew about land, and its
occupation. He knew that if the parish which he started were
ever to be worthy of its name, it needed an honest-to-goodness
church, and not just the all-purpose room that served as church
on Sunday and weekday mornings, as school auditorium during
the day—and then, on weekend nights, as a dance hall for the
teens.

 ·   Nowadays it would be called "multi-use," but in those
days it was just plain smart for him to raise as much money as
he could by using the existing structures to build the church of
his dreams. The teen dances could clear several thousand dollars
in one weekend, thanks to the volunteer staff of chaperons and
coat checkers.

My mother was one of these volunteers. When she worked
with the coats, I had a chance to cruise for chicks, though her
presence did cramp my style a little. But when she was a
chaperon, the night was lost. I would never be able to pick a girl
up with my mother right there. And I couldn't engage in the
dances called the Grind or the Dirty Dig—not that I really

would have anyway, I was too young to really get the point about the pleasure of leg grinding. My mother's presence certainly made it not an option.

There were three nights' worth of dancing on a weekend, with different age groups targeted for different nights. The seventh- and eighth-graders would come on Friday night, high schoolers on Saturday night, and "young adults"—kids who had either graduated or flunked out of high school but were supposedly over eighteen—on Sunday nights.

The liturgical purity of the sanctuary was maintained by closing the proscenium curtain, thus separating the altar area from the main hall. All the chairs, steel though portable, were taken up by the sexton on Friday afternoon, sometimes with the help of the eighth-grade boys. The American and Vatican flags, however, were kept in place, on either side of the stage apron.

The music came from 45s played by a disc jockey on a table set in front of the stage. Some of the teen dances in the area sported a DJ who had become a personality by doing a radio show. Hy Lit and Jerry Blavat each had his own teen dance, but at Holy Cross the host was anonymous, though he played the best music imaginable—sometimes in exactly the same order, week after week, always ending with three slow songs at the end, which inevitably included "All in the Game." Even today I can't hear that song without thinking of the dances at Holy Cross, and even the very area where I would be during the final sequence, back by the right-hand-side confessionals.

When referring to the space as a church, we called it Holy Cross, but when referring to the place as a dance space, it was simply "the Cross."

For a Protestant, the sentence "Are you going to the Cross this weekend?" might sound like an invitation to repent of one's sins, but for us it had more to do with an invitation to commit some. Not that dancing was forbidden by the Catholic church, as it was by some of the Protestant churches, but dancing might be, for some especially scrupulous souls (like myself), an Occasion of Sin. The phrase *occasion of sin* comes from the catechism, and denotes any person, place, or thing that could lead to—or *occasion*—the committing of sin, while not *causing* it to occur. This type of Jesuitical distinction is the secret of the old Catholic education—it gave your imagination good exercise, both by providing such distinctions and letting thoughts come to the surface that might be sins in themselves.

A sin can be a thought, word, or deed, or even an omission, that hurts God. I'm not sure what it would mean to hurt God, but I do know I've had thoughts that I considered wrong—usually after the fact—and insofar as the Cross might have given some people a chance to think impure thoughts about certain other people, I suspect it could have been an occasion of sin, but not for me. All right, so my mother was there a lot, but not always, and any thoughts I might have had were perfectly gentlemanly. Besides, the area I preferred was right near the confessionals, and the Stations of the Cross (graphic bas-relief plaques depicting the Passion and Death of Christ) surrounded the entire hall, reminding us of the consequence of our sin, no matter how private.

There were two main styles of dance and dress in those days. There was the Jive crowd, and the Conservative one. I used to think that it was a racial issue—the members of the Jive group were Italians, the Conservatives Irish—but my sister fell in with the Jive crew, and she was the same race as I, sort of Irish. I was allowed to be pegged in a subset of the Conservative—i.e., Collegiate. It didn't necessarily mean you were going to college, though that probably helped; it had more to do with style of dress and presentation. I was the right size for it—skinny—and in fact I did decide to go to St. Joseph's College because the school colors suited my wardrobe, since my favorite sweater color was maroon.

The male members of the Jive set kept their hair greased up in pompadours and ducktails and wore tighter clothing—peg-legged pants, leather jackets, sunglasses. The Conservatives wore their hair short and pressed down to the side; although grease was also allowed, Brylcreem usually did the trick. The quintessential sign of the Collegiate, though, was the tucked-in sweater, preferably V-neck.

The girls of the former tribe wore their hair in beehives or other forms of "teased" hair, tight and sometimes revealing clothing—especially sheer white blouses that revealed the bra line—and sometimes higher heels. The Conservative girls wore plaid skirts and sweaters that buttoned all the way to the neck. The quintessential Conservative and Collegiate girl wore a pin at her neck, a circle pin made from small scarabs, sometimes given to her by a boyfriend, her wearing it sometimes a sign of commitment.

Preparation to go to the Cross dances began after dinner on a Saturday night by turning the radio on to WHAT-FM, 96.5, a great jazz station. Thanks to my Aunt Bet, who had given me a portable AM-FM radio for my graduation from eighth grade, I could listen to the show, which helped me mentally prepare for the night ahead, as I physically prepared with a shower and then faced the mirror for final touches.

Although there was little to shave from my face, I went through the motions, ending with a splash of Aqua Velva, which always burned wonderfully. My father used Old Spice, and I did too when I was younger, but Aqua Velva was a sign of my independence from him, and a sign, so I thought, of my youth.

My hair was shampooed with a product called Enden, which kept unsightly dandruff from gracing my shoulders, but what went on top of it was a variety of products throughout my adolescence.

When I was in grade school, the fashion was to have a pompadour, a little wave in the front of the hairline. My hair was very thin, and so keeping a wave in the front took some doing. The most effective product, I found, was a pomade called Olivo. It was a green, thick substance that came in a little plastic jar that could be found in the women's toiletries section of the five-and-ten.

By high school, however, the task (for a Conservative Collegiate like myself) was keeping the hair straight across on the head, no pompadour, and for this other ointments were more useful. Wildroot Cream Oil was a white lotion that was heavy enough to keep down my cowlicks, but Vitalis felt like a more grown-up product. For smell and style, however, nothing beat Brylcreem. Their advertising on TV was the sexiest, with a girl running her hand through an actor's hair without getting sticky. It came in a tube and was lighter than the other products, so it didn't always hold down my back cowlick, but with care and attention, the job could be done. Of all of these scents, however, the Enden was the most powerful, leaving a dandruff-fighting residue that made its use worthwhile.

I can't imagine what I must have smelled like, really. There were a lot of scents emanating from my teenage body. It's a wonder I could smell my dance partners. I'm sure they could smell me.

I always had several pairs of dark dress pants to choose from, and black socks, of course, always black socks. Not because they matched my black military (in deference to my father) shoes, but because they were the emblem of the Conservative look. A boy at Holy Cross dances who wore white socks with dark pants and shoes was an obvious fool, and the accepted butt of jokes. Even today, I see this decision as either foolish or very bold. So pervasive was the black socks rule that articles in the newspaper outlining their health risks were widely ignored in favor of style.

I was lucky that the Cross was the dance hall of choice among my peers. It was around the corner from our house, so I didn't need a car or a ride to get there. I would leave the house a few moments before seven-thirty (after my mother had left, never with her, although sometimes I walked home with her, after everyone else had gotten their coats and gone) and walk two hundred yards to line up to be among the first inside. Invariably I would hook up with someone I knew in the line, so I always had someone to hang out with at the Cross.

I was also lucky that I was a good dancer and accepted by my peers as such. It was the era of "American Bandstand," after all, and dancing was a skill that was respected, even among boys. After this era, this was not so much the case, and by the time I was chaperoning dances myself as a high school teacher, few of the boys could dance (or chose to). My parents were dancers, and besides the benefits of genetics, I had had some good lessons from my mother, especially in the art of the jitterbug.

In high school, the Holy Cross dance would become the center of the social life among the kids I knew. Since very rarely would one bring a date to the dance, the dance floor was a place for searching for a new girlfriend, or trying to cement relationships that were tentative. A girl's decisions about whom to dance with were watched closely by all of her girlfriends, as well as by any boy who might be interested in setting up a relationship with her. It was here that dance styles would be tried for compatibility, and here that dates could be set, though never a date to go to the dance itself. These maneuvers were made somewhat more complex when the event expanded to include two spaces on different floors, the upstairs cafeteria space and downstairs church hall space. Thus a girl who wanted to play two sets of flirtations had an easy time of it.

One Saturday night in my junior year, a night when my mother couldn't make it, I had my heart broken by a pretty girl whom I had sort of been chasing named Terry Hartnett. I say "sort of" chasing, because I could never make up my mind in those days about which girl I really wanted to be with. Many of them hung out together, making things more complex. The fact that Terry and Kathy Hughes, the girl that I would later take to the junior prom, shared a back yard between their respective houses made things even trickier.

At this particular time, I tended to hang out upstairs in the cafeteria section. It was newer and novel, and less crowded than downstairs. I had danced a few dances in the earlier part of the night with Terry, and then she went downstairs—disappeared on me, as it were. I stayed upstairs with the kids that she came with, Joanne Cunningham and some others, and didn't think too much about it, knowing that Terry would come back sooner or later, at least to get a ride with her friends. When she did come back, however, toward the end of the night, it was with the announcement that she was getting a ride with someone else—a kid from St. James, a rival boys' high school. I was crushed. It served me right, of course, because I had not pursued her hard enough.

And so for revenge, I decided I would come on strong to another girl, someone to whom I would never have paid attention if it weren't for such an ulterior motive as revenge. It would be as close to sinning as I would come at the Cross.

Her name was Edie Nevits, and she was stacked, as we used to say. She was fairly cute, and considered a little cheap, meaning that she was freer with her corporal sovereignty than most of the other girls I knew. She was also a classmate of Terry's, though the two didn't really hang out much together when they were outside of school. As soon as Terry made her announcement, looking at me out of the corner of her eye, I made my move, hoping that Terry would see it. Edie was standing near the concession stand, with some of the other girls of less repute, and I walked over and grabbed her hand.

"Put down your Coke and dance with me," I said in a voice with strength born of hurt.

She took a last swallow, and came out onto the floor. The dance was a jitterbug, and I saw Terry's last glance back at us before she left the upstairs room. My plan was working. The next record was slow, and I asked her to dance again. She consented. Her hair was a little teased, affixed with hairspray that stung my eyes, and she wore more makeup that I would have preferred, but I held her close, both my arms around her, as opposed to my normal way of dancing, in the ballroom position, one hand held high and apart from the body. She responded in kind, which surprised me, and I almost panicked for a moment, not knowing if I could really pull off my plan—or whether I really wanted to. After another slow dance, I made my move, actually surprising myself when I asked her, "Would you like to see the sacristy?"

The sacristy was the room behind the sanctuary, where the altar boys prepared for Mass. In it were kept the cassocks and surplices, water and wine, and the candlelighter. It could be reached by slipping through a side door right off the corridor connecting the upstairs hall with the downstairs. My plan was to take her there and see what would happen. Even if nothing happened, just going there with her would be enough revenge on Terry.

"Sure," she said, cracking her gum loudly, a practice that separated her from girls like Terry, "but are we allowed to go there now?" I knew she was thinking, *Are girls allowed there at all?* So was I, to tell the truth.

"Don't worry, I'll get us in," I said, avoiding the ethical aspect of her question by focusing on the technical problem. I wasn't actually sure I could get us in. It all depended on whether the door was unlocked, which it usually was. It was the one used by the altar boys for school-day masses. Only those who were supposed to ever used it, and the numinous nature of what lay behind normally kept anyone else from even trying it.

We went down the stairs and stopped on the landing with the door. After making sure no one was coming, I tried the knob. It turned and in a second we were inside the darkness, the smell of candle wax and old incense filling our nostrils.

"What's that smell?" she asked.

"Candles mostly, never been back here before?" I responded.

"Never," she said, appropriately dazed by our daring.

"There's a light around here somewhere," I whispered, feeling along the wall for a switch, lighting the kitchen, with its refrigerator and sink. Beyond the other door was the altar boys' sacristy.

She walked over to the fridge. "What's in here?" she asked dumbly. Before I could answer or, more importantly, stop her, the door creaked open, revealing two bottles of Tokay altar wine, one sealed, the other a quarter full. She reached in and grabbed the open one, unscrewed the top, and took a drink, just like that.

What am I getting myself into? I wondered as she handed me the bottle. I raised it to my lips but kept them closed, knowing it would be a definite sin for me, an altar boy, but not wanting to spoil the moment for her. I took the cap from her hand and screwed it back on, and returned the bottle, trying to wipe the lipstick from the top as I did and wondering what the next morning's altar boy would think if he saw the red residue.

"Did you ever wear a cassock and surplice?" I asked.

She looked truly shocked at the suggestion, then smiled at the thought and said, "Not yet."

"Come with me."

We entered the next room, and I turned on the light, revealing the racks of red robes and white blousy tops, some hung neatly, some hung over the top of the rack itself. I chose a short cassock, and held it out to her, my heart beating hard in my chest, hoping that she would turn down the offer of this sacrilege. But the Tokay was working; with a flushed face, she said, "Turn around."

My knees began to shake. I turned around, and was surprised when her blouse fell over my head, the smell of her perfume drowning me in fear and anticipation. It was too late to explain to her that you kept your shirt on under the cassock, at least we altar boys did, and I took her blouse and folded it over my arm and waited while she buttoned the thirty-nine buttons in the front of the garment.

"No peeking," she tormentingly chanted. I heard her go over to the surplice rack and put on one of these.

"All right, turn around."

When I did, what I saw was the greatest visual argument against female priests that anyone can imagine. Her breasts filled the garments wonderfully, and I felt a tingle down my spine and beyond. A voice inside my head was screaming, *Get out now, get out right now before you are condemned to Hell for all eternity.*

"Here," I said quickly, "get dressed." I handed her the blouse and tried to escape back into the kitchen.

"Not so fast, altar boy," she said, blocking my path.

"Please, get dressed, we have to get out of here, someone might come."

"Dance with me" was her only reply, as she flung her blouse onto the rack of cassocks and grabbed my hands. Figur-

ing that humoring her for a moment might advance my cause
in the long run—my new cause, that is, not the original one that
had resulted in this mess—I held her and danced a few steps,
thankful that the strangeness of the situation had relativized my
desire, which was no longer in physical evidence, thank Heaven.
After a few rocks back and forth, I said, "It's almost time for
the mixer to end. You don't want to be locked in here, do you?"

The thought woke her up. "No, I'll miss my ride, but kiss
me first."

I kissed her quickly, handed her back the blouse, and
bolted into the kitchen, wiping off her garish lipstick. A few
moments later, she followed, dressed though a little disheveled.
I tried to unmuss her hair as best I could. I went into the other
room to turn the lights off, noticing the lipstick stain on the
cassock and wondering how Sunday's altar boy would appre-
ciate the scent of her perfume. I guided her to the exit, turning
the kitchen light out and motioning her to wait quietly while I
pulled open the door a crack.

A few chaperons and a lot of kids were descending the
stairs; the dance was ending for the night. I opened the door
quickly and pushed her out, following a second later, to the
surprised looks of some kids I (luckily) didn't know. We went
back upstairs.

Her friends were smirking as she joined them. She turned
back to me. "Thanks for the dance, Father Stivender," she said
coyly. I just nodded and smiled wanly, glad to have escaped
what might have been a real Occasion of Sin, not really caring
if the report got back to Terry to make her jealous, thankful to
have escaped the jaws of Hell and lived.

At Confession the following Saturday, I had to repeat the
episode several times, and couldn't help noticing the priest's
voice was punctuated by what was either laughter or a persist-
ent cough.

Learning to Drive

*M*y father returned from the Navy for a spell in my senior year. Just long enough to teach me to drive.

Up to that point we had had a number of cars, the most notable being a '57 Chevy, blue on blue on blue. With the distinctive Chevy fins of that year, a dashboard with futuristic air vents, and cloth and leather upholstery, it was a classic. But within a year he sold it to put some money into the downtown health club that he and his partner had so far failed to develop into the booming business he had hoped for. It would have been a great car for a high school kid to have access to, but it was not to be.

The car Dad got when he was stateside this one particular time was a beauty in its own right. It was a boat, as my friend Ed Deegan would call similar cars of a later day. The interior felt like the lobby of a hotel—cloth seats, vibrant dashboard sporting a clock with radium dials that glowed in the dark.

It was a Pontiac Super Chief sedan. A tan and white two-toned boat sedan, with the Indian head on the trunk door, and an aggressive front grille that sported boob bumpers—not as big as those on the Cadillacs of the time, but serious looking nonetheless.

It was probably not the ideal car for learning to drive, as big as it was, but that didn't matter to me. I was glad he was home for a while, and just in time to teach me.

It was November of 1963, and we had made a date for the Sunday before Thanksgiving for the lesson. The plan was to take the car to the Acme food store parking lot for the beginning of the lesson, until I figured out how to handle it and parallel park, and then take a ride into the country, Norristown to be exact, to visit his partner.

But then two days before, Friday the 22nd, President Kennedy was assassinated.

We were at the end of Religion class when we heard the news. An announcement came over the PA system to the effect that the president had been shot. Then the bell rang to change classes, and we were on our way to gym. My friend Vince Morgan and I walked together in a daze.

Vince and I hung around together that year. He was the most musically aware kid in my section. He had introduced me to the music of Bob Dylan a few months before, and we used to go to coffeehouses downtown together. He had an anti-establishment streak in him that made us great friends. We were always the last ones in line for whatever gym ignominy they had planned for us, and I would try to emulate his Olympian attitude toward the teachers and other students, though I didn't have the nose for it. He did.

We walked from Religion class to gym together. Quietly. In fact, the entire school was quiet. The hallways between periods at Bonner were usually noisy, hectic places, with Student Guards to keep the traffic flowing and watch for infractions on the up-the-down-staircase rule. Often the entire student body would take up the sound of cattle, mooing loudly as we edged our way around the guards and up and down the stairs.

But today it might as well have been a May Procession, or a funeral. There was no noise at all. Here and there boys would look at each other and mouth the word *shot* with a look of disbelief or despair. As Catholics, we were invested in the success of President Kennedy. He had dispelled the Protestant suspicions about treasonous allegiance to the Pope and had made Catholicism an acceptable mode of American life. He had given every one of us a sense of hope in the future. If this Catholic could be president, then, by golly, so could I, we all knew or thought or felt on some deep level. Now that hope was dashed.

As we made our way to the locker room, I was hoping Morgan would have some wit to dispel the gloom, but even he was oppressed by it. We all were. The locker room, usually the site of hazing and torture by bullies and jocks, was quiet as we all changed our clothes. The gym teacher's voice, trying to get us moving, was the only sound, but even his voice didn't have the edge it normally had. He knew he wasn't going to get the enthusiasm from us that he needed to make his job go smoothly.

Usually he had basketballs, ropes, soccer balls ready for us, at least those of us who liked that sort of thing. That was one good thing about gym at Catholic school, you could hang to the side if you wanted and only participate when forced, but today he knew that everyone was for hanging to the side.

We slowly filed out to the gym floor, heads hung low, guys talking to themselves, and waited for his instructions.

"We're gonna run today boys, run, all right, out the door, here we go ..."

And then the PA crackled into life, and everyone stopped and held his breath.

"Gentlemen," came the principal's voice, "we have just received word that at one-twenty-six today, President John F.

Kennedy died of wounds from a bullet to the head. May the souls of the faithful departed rest in peace."

"Amen," said those of us who could speak.

And then we all went for the door. I looked at Morgan. Tears were beginning to form, but he turned away from me and out the door. I followed, torn between wanting to cry out loud and not wanting my peers to see me do so.

Running turned out to be the perfect solution to a difficult moment. The only rational thing any of us could do was run, just as hard as we could. Three hundred boys took the field and began to run, some choking on tears, some boxing an invisible opponent as they ran, some stopping suddenly to shout their anger at no one there, then rejoining the pack of seniors, wounded in the heart. Camelot was over, Kennedy was dead. Of course we all ran too fast and were winded early, but at least we didn't cry openly in front of one another like the kids in last-period Trig or French must have. When we were all too tired to run anymore, we were signaled back inside with the whistle.

Soon we were on our way home. The girls at the trolley stop were crying their eyes out and hugging one another. No flirting with the Bonner boys that day.

Later, at dinner, I tentatively brought up the subject of the scheduled driving lesson. It wasn't that I didn't want to honor Kennedy, but I wasn't sure when my dad would be redeployed, and I didn't want to blow this chance to learn to drive.

"Sure son, no problem, as long as you've got your learner's permit." As a Protestant, he wasn't as affected by the tragedy as the rest of his family. For once I was glad of his tradition, that it didn't make him feel that the weekend should be devoted to stationary mourning.

When I rose on Sunday, my sorrow about Kennedy was overshadowed by my excitement. I was a little nervous about what lay ahead. My father was very demanding, in general, and I needed his approval. As I washed and dressed, I thought about how I could disappoint him. In school I was very bright, and my marks were never a problem between us, but driving, I wasn't so sure it was going to be all fun. At least I was getting it done and could join the ranks of my friends who already had their licenses.

I did have a little experience behind the wheel. My Aunt Bet had taken me out in her Corvair one time. The summer just past I had driven Kathy Hughes's parents (brand new) car up on Hartnetts' lawn, missing a tree and some shrubbery by a few feet, but I blamed it on the stiff steering mechanism, and her parents never found out about it (till now). Their car was much smaller than the one I would be working with this day, however.

When I came home from church, my dad was sitting at the dining room table eating his favorite Sunday breakfast, eggs and canned salmon. This salmon was the only real indulgence my father afforded himself that the family did not also share. I don't remember ever tasting canned salmon for breakfast. I always assumed it was a Southern thing—he had grown up in South Carolina—and I was too Yankified to understand it.

I went into the kitchen and kissed my mother. Her eyes were red—from crying about Kennedy, I figured. She hugged me, a bit too hard.

"Too bad about Kennedy, huh?"

She nodded, biting her lower lip.

"Bacon and eggs, Eddie?" she asked, after a deep shaky breath.

I felt bad that she was waiting on me in this condition, but I rationalized that waiting on me would take her mind off her grief.

"Yes, please, and toast, real butter please." I was the only one in the family who could tell the difference between butter and oleomargarine, or at least the only one to whom it mattered. Its existence in the house was an indulgence for me, perhaps an overindulgence.

"Hi, Dad," I said, taking my place at the table. I didn't kiss him, although I was very glad to have him home.

"Good morning, son, are you ready for your driving lesson?"

"Yes sir, ready as I'll ever be, I guess." I looked at the headlines of the paper he held.

"They caught the guy, huh?" I asked.

"Looks like, a Commie sympathizer named Lee Harvey Oswald." He held the paper so I could read the headline clearly. There was a picture of the front of the hospital in Dallas with limos and cop cars. "I wonder how Marilyn feels now."

"Oh, Alvey," scolded my mother, though the comment went right over my head, "is nothing sacred to you?" She placed a plate before me with two pieces of toast. I picked one up to taste the yellowish pats melting on one side. Butter. I could always tell because of the way it coated the tongue.

"Just three things, my dear—thee, the sea, and G-O-D." He tried to give her a hug from his sitting position, but she hit him away kiddingly with the dish towel and returned to the kitchen.

This moment seemed to cheer her up a bit. I was glad. She returned a moment later with two perfect eggs and two strips of bacon. She always claimed that it was all in the frying pan and none of her doing. The frying pan was a phenomenal one, black cast iron with the memory of thousands of meals crusted on its exterior, but it was her timing with an egg that made it right.

"Thanks, Mom, it looks great."

"Do you want orange juice?"

"Please." We always had frozen orange juice, thanks to an amazing frozen food plan that came as an option with the Renaire refrigerator-freezer that we had. Every two weeks, a uniformed guy would come to the house and stock the freezer that made up the lower half of the unit with all kinds of food, all frozen—meat, vegetables, and juices that filled the racks in the door.

She returned with the red metal pitcher that condensed so well in the summertime and filled my waiting glass.

"Alvey?"

"No, thanks, Anne, I will have some coffee, though."

I was glad he had coffee, so I didn't have to rush my breakfast, but sad at the same time because he might delay our adventure with the slowness of his sips. I was never satisfied.

"Why do you think he did it, Dad?"

"I don't know, son."

"Well, Johnson has a hard road ahead of him," said my mother, wistfully as she cleared the dishes.

"And so do we, son, so we better get going if we're gonna make a showing," he said as he folded the newspaper and rose to help my mother. "You'll be all right without your men today, won't you, Annie Rooney?" he kiddingly asked, using his pet name for her.

"I'll be all right as long as you bring my son back safe."

"Don't worry, hon, all the assassins are off today."

The thought of a marksman shooting at us as we drove chilled my heart for a moment, but at least I didn't have to think about the possibility that was really on my mother's mind. *Son Kills Father and Self in Fiery Crash.* Whew.

"Oh, Alvey," she chided as he hugged her goodbye. "Where are you going to go?"

"First to the Acme parking lot for turning and parking and then out to Norristown to drop in on Jake," he replied.

"Not that Jake," she groaned.

"There's nothing wrong with that Jake, he's my business partner, and I want Eddie to meet him."

The health spa business did not meet with my mother's approval. She always assumed something shady was going on downtown, and she was angry that she couldn't see much of a return for my father's investment of time and money.

"Eddie, if he asks you for any of your Bible money, don't give it to him." I had worked that summer selling Bibles door-to-door, and still had about two hundred in the bank.

"Don't worry, Mom, not a chance," I said, kissing her on the cheek. She hugged me too hard again, and I got the sense that she was really worried about us. Or at least about me.

"Wear your heavy coat, it's cold out there today."

"Yes, ma'am," said the obedient son, knowing that the coat would come off as soon as I was a block from the house. It would interfere with my driving, after all.

"Will you be back in time for dinner?"

"We'll be home before dark."

"Be careful."

We walked down the steps to the car. I waited for my father to gesture where I would sit. He handed me the keys and said, "Open the passenger side first, you sit in the driver's seat."

"C.Y.K.," called my mother from the doorway. It was family code for Consider Yourself Kissed.

I let my father in the passenger's side and went around to the driver's side waving as I walked. "C.Y.K.," I returned.

"I'm too nervous to watch," she said—to herself, but loud enough for me to hear—and went back inside. At least that pressure was off.

I unlocked the car door and slid into the driver's seat, my heart pounding.

"The ignition is right here, put the key in, but don't start it up yet."

I obeyed.

"The first thing you want to do when you are in a car that's new to you is sit and get used to it," he began, speaking in a tone that let me know this was a lesson. I sat back, my eyes just a little higher than the dashboard. My feet could touch the pedals, but just barely.

"There's a lever underneath the seat that you can push to move it up."

I felt around for it and pushed it, and the seat jumped back a notch. The seat was one of those long hotel-lobby couch things.

"All right, that's the lever, now pull it up and we'll both move forward and it will follow. One, two, three."

The seat went forward a little too far. One more time and we had it. I could see and touch the pedals fully.

"Comfortable?"

"Yes, sir."

"Next step, find the headlight switch."

This part was easy, actually, given the fact that I had tried every button in the car one day, unbeknownst to him, but I knew that this drill would do me good. I pretended to search, found the knob and pulled it.

"Very good, now, turn on the bright lights."

I looked down at my feet and pushed the button on the floor. I heard a click, but could see no difference, as the daylight made the results of the exercise invisible.

"Now turn it off."

Click.

"Now turn the headlights off completely."

I pushed in the button on the dashboard.

"Very good, son."

I smiled, thankful for his approval, glad the first test had gone well. The rest of the preparatory drill included windshield wipers, heater, gear shift (it was automatic, so there was no clutch to worry about), turn signals (in those days you had to know the hand signals as well to pass the driver's test), and finally radio.

"Now start the car by pumping the gas pedal twice and holding it halfway down, then turning over the ignition. Try it."

My Guardian Angel must have been on duty, because the car started right up.

"Now put it into Drive, the red D on the steering column, while keeping your right foot on the brake. Always use your right foot in an automatic, so when you learn standard you can use your left foot for the clutch."

I did as he said, and when the car lurched slightly as it got in gear, I knew this was the real thing. I was finally driving.

"Look out your rearview mirror to make sure no one is coming, and press down slowly on the gas."

I fought my tendency to turn around to see if anyone was coming and pressed down. The car lurched ahead, and I was driving down Springfield Road, heart in my throat, sweaty hands on the wheel.

"Are you all right, son?" he asked.

"I'm fine," I said, thankful for the chance to lie myself into truth, happy that I was finally on my way, my ecstasy at being on an adventure with my dad tempered by the fear of failure.

"Shall I turn on the radio?" he asked, sensing from the sight of my white knuckles that I wouldn't have a free hand for this task, at least not right then. There was no music on any of the stations, just up-to-the-minute reports from announcers who all seemed to be choked up by the events of the day. Lee Harvey Oswald was in jail and would be moved later on for a hearing, and now back to our anchor in Washington for an update on the Kennedy family ... He turned it off.

By the time we got to the Acme, I was feeling almost comfortable. Since it was Sunday, the store was closed, so the lot was empty and smooth. Parallel parking turned out to require more strength than I had figured, and soon my left arm was aching a little, but I learned the distances and angles quickly, with his help and the help of some shopping baskets that he called into service, and soon we were on our way to Norristown to visit Jake. I was beginning to feel exhilarated.

Route 202 was a pretty good highway, two lanes in each direction for much of the way, and it went through beautiful countryside. At one point, I had to get into the right-hand lane and made the mistake of turning around in my seat to see if there was anything coming. I was surprised and unnerved by my father's angry response to the gaffe. It has stayed with me to this day. I rarely change lanes even now without thinking of him. But other than that one mistake, the drive went well.

Following his directions, I pulled the car up in front of a white clapboard house with a porch, very glad that I didn't have to try my new-found skill of parallel parking so soon after acquiring (or nearly acquiring) it. I turned the car off and dutifully checked all the buttons and levers to make sure nothing was left on to drain the battery.

A man with a mustache, a cigar in his mouth, appeared on the porch. A dog ran beside him, wagging his tail, anxious to sniff us as we went up the stairs.

"He won't bite," said our host, reiterating the pet owner's myth from antiquity. I petted the mutt cautiously, more to be a good guest than from any love of animals.

"Jake," said my father, "this is my son, Eddie."

I put my hand out to shake his. It was a salesman's grip, too sincere.

"Nice to meet you, kiddo, your father has told me all about you. Come on in, we're watching the TV. They're gonna have the assassin on in a second, they're moving him to a courtroom or something. Creepy looking guy."

Our host opened the door and I entered, my father right behind. The television was visible as soon as we got inside the door. The volume was turned down, but we could see a corridor with policemen and guys in hats waiting. Jake closed the door behind us and motioned us to sit down on the couch, but before we could do so, Oswald appeared on the screen.

"There he is," said Jake. We watched as he came down the hall toward the camera.

"Looks too skinny to be an assassin, eh?" said Jake.

I didn't say anything. I was pretty skinny myself and didn't really know how to respond. There was no pressure, though, it was a rhetorical question.

As we watched the skinny guy being brought down the hall of the police station, a guy with a hat came in from the lower right-hand side of the screen. Suddenly, the skinny guy fell and there was chaos and shouting, and it became clear that the assassin himself had been shot.

I took a seat on the couch, and the three of us stared, amazed, at the TV screen.

"Well, there it is," said our host. "Now we'll never know why he did it. Eddie, want some lemonade?"

I looked at my father for a cue before I answered yes.

"Alvey, how 'bout a beer?"

"Sure, Jake."

I was surprised at how quickly Jake turned from viewing a national tragedy to serving his guests, and wasn't sure I disagreed with my mother in her dislike of this guy.

Jake and my father talked all afternoon while I read magazines and watched the TV, the shooting of Oswald playing over and over. It wasn't till later that I realized how lucky I was to learn how to drive on that day, since there were fewer cars on the road than normal, everybody being home at the TV, involved in mourning, and now viewing a second death, one that didn't deserve tears but was strange nonetheless.

When we finally left Jake's, the sun had gone down, so my father drove back. I was afraid we would be late for dinner, but he had called right before we left, and when we did arrive, the dinner was still hot.

I was glad to be home, safe and sound. I hadn't crashed the car, we hadn't been shot at—though someone had been—and I knew I'd pass the driver's test the following Wednesday. My mother was glad to see us, and she hugged me too hard for the third time that day.

Still Catholic
After All These Fears

Winning the debate against Brumfield (albeit by default) had put me in an interesting position in an exciting period of the Church's history. The previous November, Pope John XXIII had promulgated a constitution of the Second Vatican Council, changing the practice and language of the Mass for the first time in four hundred years. By my senior year, as I was trying to disprove the existence of God, the Mass was being said in English, the organ was ignored in favor of guitars, and people at church were noticing their neighbors in the pew.

I was appalled.

My atheism notwithstanding, I was still a conservative Catholic, and my conservatism was under attack from the very quarters that should have been defending it: the hierarchy.

After my first experience with an English-language Mass the summer before my senior year, I dashed out to the record store to buy LPs with librettos in the old language, doing my part to preserve the heritage that had brought such joy to my youth as an altar boy. It was a very important shopping spree, yielding the twelfth-century *Play of Herod,* which is still dear to me, as well as my all-time favorite, *Carmina Burana,* with Eugene Ormandy conducting the Philadelphia Orchestra, and a chorus singing bawdy and often untranslatable lyrics written by defrocked Benedictine monks. I cared little what the content was—at least it was in Latin.

Coming out of the store, I met an old friend of my mother's who had babysat me as an infant. I still called her by her nickname, "Dodo," even though she was by that time a Sister of Notre Dame. I explained to her the nature and motive of my purchases, and I still remember her look of pity—and my horror that a woman as old as my mother was supportive of changes that would, I was sure, destroy the Church.

The dropping of Latin had the effect of pulling the rug out from under some of us who had spent so much time learning the old ways. As an altar boy I had worked hard at my role, respondent at the altar of God. Now I felt that the Church was no longer in need of my services, and I was being retired at the ripe age of seventeen. I can't imagine how some of the older priests must have felt.

But the elimination of Latin wasn't the only change. Much more disturbing were the new additions—for instance, the "Kiss of Peace." This gesture was not so much a new thing as a revival of an old custom that St. Paul talks about in one of his epistles. It could be detected in the old Latin Mass when the priest, while secretly breaking the bread and dropping a piece of it into the cup of wine—with his back to the congregation but loud enough for the altar boys to hear—said, while blessing the cup, "*Pax Domini sit semper vobiscum*" ("the peace of the Lord be always with you") to which the altar boy responded: "*et cum spiritu tuo*" ("and with your spirit," or "and also with you").

This was all part of the hushed period just before the priest's and our communion, a most private time of the Mass when the people were most interiorly directed in preparation for reception of the host. With the changes wrought by the Second Vatican Council, this moment would become a most public one, with the priest turning toward the congregation and the congregation responding. Then the priest would issue the order: "Let us offer each other a sign of God's peace," after which we were expected to shake hands with our neighbor.

This was hitherto unheard of in modern Catholic tradition. The Mass, for better or worse, was a time of individual contemplation, a time alone with God that would give us the wherewithal to deal with our neighbor. Making this dealing with our neighbor a part of the Mass itself was a radical change in the ritual, and a distracting one at that.

Luckily for me, our pastor was even more resistant to the change than I was. As the word was coming down from Rome through the Archbishop, Father Meyer was preaching on why he was not enforcing it in his church, which basically came down to "you don't know where your neighbor's hand has been." When he finally did cave in to pressure from downtown, and the change was put in place, one's focus was diverted from attention to God to more mundane concerns (especially for an insecure adolescent): *Are my hands clammy? What if they won't shake my hand? Do I have to shake just one, or as many as I can reach? Should I cross the aisle to find a friendly hand?—or to force the issue with an unfriendly hand?* No matter what, it broke the spell that had developed during the earlier part of the Mass. Later on in some congregations, especially the Pentecostal and socially active ones, this moment would become (perhaps appropriately so) the prolonged center of the celebration, not ending until everyone had shaken every hand in the room. But at Holy Cross it was a long time coming—luckily for some of us.

Although it may seem strange for a person to be a free thinker in philosophy, and an ultraconservative in practice, it has always been the case with me. The realm of the sacred is such a tender and tenuous place, fraught with doubts and paradox, that I have always appreciated a rigidity of form, which is liberating in the long run. The fact that my public self at school was that of an atheist and my private self was that of a dyed-in-the-wool conservative, made my crisis of faith more than usually complex and influenced to a great degree my choice of a college. It had to be Catholic, it had to be conservative, it had to be inexpensive.

Very few of my classmates at Msgr. Bonner High School chose secular institutions for post-secondary study. There were stories about older brothers who had tried, only to find that their applications or recommendations had mysteriously disappeared after they had given them to the guidance counselors to be sent along. Among the guidance staff there was clearly a bias toward good Catholic institutions over possible dens of iniquity and/or Communism like Penn or Swarthmore.

For me, it was either Villanova or St. Joseph's College. I never really considered any others. Some of my friends were going to LaSalle, the other Catholic college in Philadelphia, but it had a reputation of being too liberal. Besides, I really liked St. Joseph's colors: crimson and gray, translated in popular fashion to maroon and gray, which matched my casual wardrobe, such as it was, at the time.

St. Joseph's was run by Jesuits, and everyone knew their reputation as scholars and learned men. Villanova would have meant four more years of Augustinians, and I wanted to expand my intellectual horizons to include another order.

Perhaps the bottom line, however, was the bottom line— St. Joe's was cheaper. For $950 per year, you could get a Jesuit education—if you commuted, which everybody did. The college had two old buildings that served as dorms for at the most fifty kids, but everybody else took public transportation, or drove their dad's car, or carpooled, or hitchhiked.

My parents couldn't really afford to send us to college, so I had to borrow the money through the wonderful, though now defunct, National Defense Education Act. This act enabled the government to guarantee any bank loan made for educational purposes, which made the loans easy to get. The borrowed money could be used not only for tuition but also for living expenses and books. Luckily, I could afford my own books with the money I made from part-time jobs, and my living expenses were paid by my long-suffering mother, who would let me stay under her roof and eat at her table as long as I (albeit begrudgingly) went to Mass every Sunday. Which I did. I may have been an atheist, but I wasn't stupid.

But first I had to be accepted, and that meant taking the "College Boards," the Scholastic Aptitude Tests developed at Princeton. Because of the number of our college-bound kids, the testing site was Bonner High School itself, thus giving me a home-field advantage.

This test was unlike any we had ever taken at school. For one thing, it had to be done in pencil, in fact two or three No. 2 pencils, that you brought with you. (Any real test at Bonner was done in pen, except for certain math tests.) Furthermore, the test answers were indicated in little square bubbles that had to be filled in completely—or erased completely.

As if it weren't already disorienting enough, the test was held on Saturday. It was given all year round, but the most popular time was in the late winter, so the scores would arrive in early spring. The cost, at that time, was five dollars.

So it was that we all gathered that Saturday morning in the lobby of the school, checked for our name on a large computerized sheet, and went to the designated room. We sat in alphabetical order in every other desk, so there would be no cheating, and were monitored by one of the teachers from the school who earned a little extra money by doing so.

I took my place with my three No. 2 pencils and waited for the rest of the group to come in. The monitor's manner was quite different from his usual classroom demeanor. He was no longer working for himself or his academic discipline, but for some higher power that had strict rules about how the morning should go in terms of time and motion. His voice had an edge it would not have had if he had been giving one of his own tests.

When everyone was seated, he handed out the answer sheets and explained how they were to be filled out. Not only would we write our name in blocks provided at the top of the page, but we would fill in blocks with our soft black pencils below. As well as our address, and in a space provided—but without connected blocks—we were to provide the name of our mother's mother. I laughed aloud at this and was scolded immediately. No explanation was given for this strange request, but I found out later it had to do with security, to keep kids from taking tests for someone else, an idea that had not occurred to me up to that time. It seemed to be a fairly flimsy security technique when I thought about it, and though I never tried to make any extra money by taking someone else's test, I always figured I could do it safely by memorizing a few genealogical facts about my patron in crime.

Once we had finished that, he handed out the test booklets, all sealed with a black paper tab. The trick of the testing game is that every participant should have the exact same experience of the test itself, so that the results are dependable. A lot was at stake for millions of kids, obviously. I found myself getting more and more serious about the task at hand as the Byzantine ritual of secrecy and timing unfolded.

The teacher kept looking at the clock, since the test was to start at nine o'clock sharp. Next to the clock was a crucifix, and I wondered if it unnerved some of the non-Catholic kids from public schools who happened to be stuck in a Catholic classroom, thanks to a computer glitch in Princeton. I knew I was fortunate to be taking the test in familiar surroundings.

The teacher was reading from a form, preparing us to get started; the clock was ticking closer and closer to nine. Finally, he said, "Begin." A flurry of paper seals ripping gave way to a worried silence of concentration as we read the first question. (Actually we were reading different questions it turns out, which I began to realize in the hall at the break, another security device. Cheaters beware.)

I read the first question and immediately relaxed. I had been taking tests like this since I was a little kid. My Aunt Fran used to receive *Parents* magazine, and I would spend a happy time on the first Saturday of the month, when the magazine came in the mail, answering the twenty or so quiz questions in the sidebar section. But even before that, there was *Children's Digest* and its quiz with the answers in the back; before that, *Humpty Dumpty's Magazine*. Taking tests was a game for me. The only difference was the dorky bubbles that had to be filled in; at least, though, that was a new challenge.

I finished before time was called, and obeyed the boldly lettered command at the bottom of the third page:

STOP! DO NOT TURN THIS PAGE
UNTIL INSTRUCTED TO DO SO.

I amused myself by trying to find patterns in the dots I had drawn on the answer sheet.

"Stop! Put your pencils down."

I jumped. The monitor's tone of voice was a bit more authoritarian than necessary.

He instructed us about the next section, which was math, and signaled the start of the test. I enjoyed the shapes that had to be matched and melded in the mind's eye. I knew how to do these from my magazine experience. I knew how to work the trains leaving at different times, meeting somewhere en route. I vaguely remembered algebraic formulas we had learned in Mr. Jost's Algebra II class, but didn't have to use them, depending instead on some line drawings I had worked up when younger. The only difficulty I had came from the strange question about filling up the swimming pool with two different hoses, one that delivered one hundred gallons a minute, the other that delivered sixty-three gallons a minute. I tried to figure out a minute-by-minute scale of delivery but got bogged down. I knew that Jost had covered this type of problem, too, but probably at the end of the term when I was suffering the symptoms of spring fever. That stupid swimming pool cost me a lot of time, and, not following the advice of the monitor to move ahead and come back to more difficult questions, I was surprised by the monitor's command and left three questions unmulled over.

It was time for a break. We all filed out into the halls and stairwells to search for friends and compare answers. These conversations were a bit frustrating when we realized that our neighbors had different tests, or at least different questions. It seemed that the SATs were cheatproof in ways that normal tests were not.

After the break we came back for more of the same. The reading comprehension was a breeze, the questions all had blinking signs pointing to the correct answer or obvious confusion points. The essay question was the most tedious, since I had to write slowly so my essay could be read (by some poor guy who must have had no life whatever, but probably was paid well for his patience) since my handwriting by that time had begun to deconstruct the Palmer Method. As much fun as it was, it was also rather exhausting, so I was glad to be finished with it.

When my test scores came back a month later, I was a little disappointed that my totals were not the perfect 800s I had hoped for, but my scores were good enough to get me accepted at Villanova and St. Joe's. I chose the latter.

St. Joseph's admissions office responded to my entrance acceptance with a letter that said that, although they could not give me any scholarship money, my NDEA loan would cover the tuition, and that I was set to be in the honors program (thanks, I think, to the input of a staunch alumnus, Debby Hanley's father). My major was to be Psychology.

The last semester of senior year was a joke, study-wise, once we got our letters of acceptance. The school play, the Bonner Fair (a carnival fund-raiser), and the senior prom claimed our attention. I never slacked off in my schoolwork enough to flunk out, but even today I have a recurring nightmare in which I am called down to the dean's office and told that I don't have enough credits to graduate, and although they may let me march in academic gown on the day of graduation, I won't get my diploma until I go to summer school.

To my prom I took Diane Kunstler, a pretty blonde Prendergast girl, who had helped me form my arguments for the debate with Brumfield. It was a more formal affair than the one in junior year, since it was held at the Ben Franklin Hotel downtown. But the formality did not dampen the dancing and fun. There were two other dances in that final high school season—Debby Hanley's senior prom, and Regina Mone's graduation dance. Regina didn't go to Prendergast. She went to Holy Child Academy, a somewhat tonier prep school. I'm not sure how we got hooked up, but I do remember feeling somewhat uncomfortable at the party afterward.

A few weeks before graduation we got our yearbooks, and spent some time thereafter getting them signed. I still have mine. I enjoy looking back at it, remembering the people who signed—and trying to figure out what creep drew a mustache and glasses on my picture.

Graduation took place at the Civic Center, the only space large enough to hold the entire class of one thousand and our families and friends. I must admit I enjoyed putting on the academic robe and mortarboard and processing in such grand style, scanning the room for my mother and sisters as I marched.

Right after graduation came Senior Week at the shore. This was the traditional time when the resorts belonged to the seniors who had been let out a week before any of the other kids. I had been going to the beach on weekends since my sophomore-year summer, using the money I earned selling Bibles door-to-door. This trip would be the most fun of all.

The New Jersey beaches were within two hours' travel by bus, and there were two resorts where most of the Bonner boys went—Wildwood and Ocean City. Wildwood was, as its name might imply, the wilder of the two, with bars that did not always card their patrons to prove age eligibility; I had gone there in the summer of my junior year, but I preferred Ocean City. It was originally incorporated as a Methodist camp meeting site, where Sunday school teachers could come for relaxation and renewal; because of this heritage, there were no bars or liquor stores, making it a safer place for families and comparative innocents like myself and my friends.

I went down with Joe Lang, John Volk, George Wargo, and some other Bonner guys. It was a spirited crew. Joe Lang had distinguished himself by hiding under the teacher's platform in Geometry class and surprising Father Zonneveld with "spirit rappings" from below. Since he was a good kid—and very smart—he had not been suspended for his pains, but no one who was present ever forgot this escapade.

John Volk was like someone out of an Evelyn Waugh novel, an aesthete and artist who would comment on the world around him with a cigarette poised between sensitive nicotined fingers. He was also a cartoonist for the Bonner paper, immortalized by his renderings of the disciplinarian, who could never escape the epithet of "Buckethead" after John's work appeared.

In this fine company, a clown like myself could have great fun. I remember one night in particular when we were cruising the boardwalk and came upon a storefront church, the last remnant of Ocean City's Methodist foundations. We watched the proceedings for a short while and then continued our walk. Cuing on the service, I began to take on the role of a messianic preacher, with a bench as my pulpit and my friends as true believing shills. It was one of my finer moments of improvisation, a prelude to what I would later do for a living.

I spent the summer working in the display department at the Lit Brothers Lawrence Park location, where Jim Kelly's father was manager and thanks to whom I had the job. I spent most of my time making signs with a primitive movable-type press and changing the clothes of mannequins on the floor. The job provided enough money for books and clothes for school—as well as a couple of additional excursions to the beach.

On my last beach excursion of the summer, I went with Tony Ercole—a friend from Havertown—and some of his friends, Bill Fletcher, Ron Gretto, Buddy Guest and Jimmy Johnson. We stayed at a popular rooming house called the St. George, in a room with three beds, so we each paid less than five dollars a night. Tony and his friends were witty guys, very relaxed with members of the opposite sex. Thanks to them, we hooked up with a group of girls, with whom we had a couple of dinners during the week.

One evening, after a spaghetti dinner with our new friends, we all went down to the boards to cruise and ended up at the Fifth Street Jetty, a pile of rocks flattened on the top that jutted out seventy yards into the ocean. At low tide it was a place for a casual stroll, at high tide it was submerged, at all tides it was a site of crashing waves and wonderful sea spray, great fun to watch. We took up our positions on the benches of the boardwalk and watched the tide coming in.

After a while, I decided to take a walk out and asked if anyone wanted to join me. No one did, involved as they were in conversation, flirting, and playing "Name A State." This game was played in pairs of opposite sex; you began with a hand on the knee of your partner and invited him or her to name a state. The state named would be incorrect, of course, allowing you to move the hand up the leg, getting closer and closer to treasure, until you blinked in this game of sexual chicken, accepting one of the states named as correct—or until your partner hit your hand away in feigned disgust. Hours of fun for the feeble-minded—or the mind made feeble by hormones.

I walked out on the jetty alone, waves crashing on either side as the tide came in. My friends were yelling to me, but I couldn't discern the message, so loud was the surf. I continued all the way to the end of the jetty, where there were railings to hold onto. The waves were getting higher and higher, but still not life-threatening. As they rolled past me, I began to notice that in their wake a great peace and quiet followed as the sea swirled and prepared the next onslaught. I looked up at the sky. The night was clear and the stars were numerous, the Big Dipper scooping light from the ferris wheels down the beach.

It was just as one of the waves was rolling past that everything changed. I experienced something that I could not name. I felt overwhelmed and safe at the same time, threatened by great power yet held in care. And connected. Connected to the sea around me and the sky above me, no difference between me and it, all of it. It was not an experience of being watched over by God or the Blessed Mother of God, as I had felt before in answer to prayers. There was no "up there" and "down here," no separation at all. I wasn't watched over, I was looked through, somehow. I wasn't more important than anything else that existed, more favored than anything or anyone, but connected—integrated to all that was there, and cared for just because I was, cared for from the inside. Often, after taking Communion (even in my atheist period), I would talk to the Lord in the Sacrament inside me, but that dialogue assumed a separation from Him. Now there was no separation, indeed now there was no need for words, no use for words.

Since reaching the Age of Reason, I had been struggling with rules and mysteries, dogmas and doctrines; I had been hounded by fears of rejection and damnation, fears about the validity of my own atheism and conservative Catholicism, fears about phoniness and authenticity. Now all these things were no longer important. Somehow I knew these feelings would return, but they would not master me. I was still Catholic after all these fears, and there was a sense of a new center that would not be washed away no matter how turbulent the tides would be. The arguments, the facades, the doubts, even the dreams didn't really matter. What mattered was the infinite care at the center.

I could see my friends watching me as I returned to the boardwalk, the water coming above my knees as I walked.

"Catch anything?" shouted one of the girls, the slightest lilt in her voice.

"Not exactly," I shouted back. "I think something caught me."

"We're going to Johnson's for ice cream, wanna come?" Tony said as I mounted the steps.

"Sure."

As we walked toward Ninth Street, I tried to explain what I felt. They all laughed good-naturedly, thinking it was another comedy routine, so I shut up. But I knew I couldn't be an atheist of fashion anymore.

The following week I would enter a Jesuit college and spend four years and seventy-two credit hours wrestling with Theology and Philosophy teachers over the words to describe what had happened and how it related to Catholic dogma in an era of change, but I knew that night that the words could not add to nor subtract from the moment.

At the ice cream parlor I had a chocolate scoop on a sugar cone, with the trademark sour ball in the bottom. How sweet it was. ❦